An Anniversary Celebration

OF SEVENTY HOMES

An Anniversary Celebration
OF SEVENTY HOMES

TEXT BY WILLIAM R. MITCHELL JR.

FOREWORD BY HARRY NORMAN

To: Dr. Betty Siegel, a great person and a super President of Kennesaw State.

Harry Norman

HARRY NORMAN, REALTORS

ATLANTA

Front and back endpaper: 555 Argonne Drive
Page 1: 555 Argonne Drive
Page 2: 555 Argonne Drive
Page 5: 207 Fifteenth Street
Pages 6-7: 10 Habersham Way, 555 Argonne Drive,
3 Cherokee Road, 155 Greenville Street
Page 8: 101 Bill Hart Road
Page 11: Harry Norman, Realtors Corporate Office
Page 13: 4135 Woodland Brook Drive
Page 176: 4270 Harris Trail

First published in 1999 by
Harry Norman, Realtors
5229 Roswell Road, NE Atlanta, Georgia 30342

MANAGING EDITOR: Amy Norman
ASSOCIATE EDITOR: Linda Williams   PROJECT EDITOR: Nancy S. Moseley
DESIGNER: Andy Sirmon

ISBN 0-9675293-0-1

Color separations and printing production in Georgia by Market Source, Inc.

Contents

Foreword
by Harry Norman

ATLANTA HOMES WERE A PART OF MY LIFE, LONG BEFORE I CONTEMPLATED REAL ESTATE AS A CAREER. MY INTRODUCTION TO MANY ATLANTA HOMES WAS AT THE AGE OF NINE WHEN I WAS STATIONED WITH A PAD AND PENCIL ON THE FRONT LAWN ACROSS THE STREET FROM MY MOTHER'S LISTINGS. MY RESPONSIBILITY WAS TO WATCH THE CARS THAT SLOWED TO LOOK AT THE HOME AND TO JOT DOWN THE LICENSE TAG NUMBERS. MY MOTHER LATER CONTACTED THE OWNERS OF THE AUTO TO SEE IF THEY WERE VIABLE PROSPECTS FOR A SALE.

That was 1930, and my mother, Mrs. Emily Norman was determined to make a change in the way residential real estate transactions were conducted in Atlanta. She and my father, a Southern Bell executive, had experienced two very unpleasant real estate dealings in the 1920s, involving misrepresentation of property and contractor negligence. These unpleasant and financially painful incidents convinced my mother that a doggedly determined and ethical salesperson could build a company and offer the people of Atlanta a desperately needed service.

There were no educational courses or licensing tests then, so with a five-dollar fee and a signed form, Mrs. Norman began her career. Real estate was a male-dominated field then, and Mrs. Norman is believed to have been the first woman licensed as a broker in Atlanta. She began selling from our home, but after a short time, she had several sales associates in her employ and she opened her first office at 77 West Paces Ferry Road. That building was torn down several years ago, but our current Buckhead office is on the same site.

I always maintained my interest in homes. I secured my real estate sales license in 1945 and went to work for my mother's company. I entered the house building business in 1950, specializing in upper-end residential properties in the Buckhead area, through 1956 when I became a partner in the firm of Mrs. Harry Norman and Associates.

"Miss Emmie" Norman continued to be very active in the company until her death in 1969 at the age of 84. Her legacy continues to flourish and prosper and is Harry Norman, Realtors today. For more than a quarter-century I served as president of Harry Norman, Realtors and in 1994 Lewis Glenn became president and chief operating officer while I moved on to become chairman of the board. I have been privileged to witness our company grow to more than 775 sales associates in 15 sales offices and divisions for Career Development, Relocation, Leasing and Property Management, and Developer Services. Sales in 1998 exceeded two and one-quarter billion dollars.

This portrait of Emily Norman, "Miss Emmie," hangs in the reception hall of the company's corporate office. Portrait by Constantine Chatov.

From the first year Miss Emmie and her white-gloved sales associates began selling homes, we became firmly established as the premier real estate company to Atlanta's carriage trade. To this day, we consistently lead in the listing and sale of the finest luxury homes in Atlanta. But as Atlanta grows, so do we, to meet the needs of our clients who buy and sell homes in all price ranges and in all areas. As the population spreads from the city center, we continue to open additional sales offices and increase our number of sales associates.

I relate all this to you so that you understand how Atlanta homes are in the very fiber of my being. For over seventy years, I have carried on more than a business relationship, but a real love affair with Atlanta homes. As a builder, I was closely involved in many of the homes in Buckhead from conception to completion. As a Realtor, I began to know more of them intimately. I watched with fascination, often in admiration, and sometimes in wonderment as subsequent owners renovated, expanded, and enhanced these same homes into the remarkable structures they are today. As a neighbor and admirer, I studied the intricacies of their architect's artistry, appreciated their uniqueness and proudly spoke of their beauty to my real estate peers around the country and the world.

In the year 2000, we will celebrate the seventieth anniversary of Harry Norman, Realtors. We aspired to offer an appropriate commemorative of our years in the community. It had to be a lasting record of the spirit and heart of the city, something we could share with the whole population and something that would be of interest to future generations.

An Anniversary Celebration of Seventy Homes was envisioned. With images in my mind of beautiful homes visited throughout seven decades, the difficulty would be in selecting only seventy homes to be photographed. These seventy are certainly among the most outstanding, and their one commonality is that during the seventy-year history of our company, we sold each of these homes at least once, some many times over.

The authorship of the book was an easy decision. When the

Georgia Trust for Historic Preservation formed the Neel Reid Educational Fund for the purpose of publishing the book *Neel Reid, Architect of Hentz, Reid & Adler and the Georgia School of Classicists*, I was pleased to join the patrons in the Neel Reid Circle. Through this project, as well as through our relationship with William R. Mitchell Jr. authoring a series of ads for us in the 1980s, I came to admire Bill Mitchell, not only for his abilities as an expert in architectural history but also for his dedication to historic preservation. William Mitchell, Georgia's well-known writer-historian and preservationist, is a native Atlantan, and an acquaintance of generations of owners of these homes; he has provided his expertise for this project.

Most importantly, this book would not have been possible but for the generosity of the owners who shared their beautiful homes with us. We thank them for allowing us to spend a full day completing our photography in each home, and for contributing to the historical details of their properties.

This book has been a labor of love. It is a pictorial chronicle of Atlanta's fine residences along with a historical chronology, a bequest to you and to future generations of Atlantans. Therefore, the proceeds from the sale of this book are being donated to the Atlanta Botanical Garden and the Southern Architecture Foundation.

I've derived a lifetime of pleasure from my acquaintance with these homes and thousands of others. In *An Anniversary Celebration of Seventy Homes*, I hope you enjoy your personal invitation to share the joy they offer.

Harry Norman

Introduction

SOON AFTER *LANDMARK HOMES OF GEORGIA* WAS PUBLISHED IN 1982, HARRY AND AMY NORMAN ASKED ME TO WRITE A SERIES OF NEWSPAPER ADVERTISEMENTS FOR HARRY NORMAN, REALTORS, FEATURING IMPORTANT HOUSES THAT THE FIRM HAD ALREADY SOLD OR WAS OFFERING FOR SALE AT THAT TIME. BEGINNING IN THE FALL OF 1983, IT TURNED OUT TO BE A POPULAR SERIES, AND IT HAS BEEN THE BASIS OF THIS BOOK PRODUCED BY HARRY NORMAN, REALTORS FOR ITS SEVENTIETH ANNIVERSARY CELEBRATION. SOME OF THE HOMES CHOSEN FOR PRESENTATION HERE WERE INCLUDED IN THAT SERIES, AMONG THEM 10 HABERSHAM WAY, WHICH IS ON THE DUST JACKET AND LOOKING BETTER THAN EVER.

Since *Landmark Homes of Georgia 1733-1983*, I have completed a number of other books. This one is my fourteenth, I am happy to report. And, I have two others in the works: *The Architecture of James Means* and *John Volk, Architect*. (Atlantans know Jimmy Means, whose work is represented here, but Volk practiced from Palm Beach, Florida, beginning in 1925.)

In April, 1998, with the help of friends, I incorporated Southern Architecture Foundation (SAF), a nonprofit, tax-deductible public charity (501,C,3). SAF's mission includes publishing handsome and popular architectural books (we hope they will be), similar to *An Anniversary Celebration of Seventy Homes*. SAF likes the association with a fine firm such as Harry Norman, Realtors, which was started seventy years ago come the year 2000.

In my little essays that accompany the beautifully photographed houses, I have emphasized location, neighborhood, context, architecture and architects, always trying to understand what various owners have done, and always being interested in accurate history, when I could obtain it. I have made numerous trips to the Atlanta History Center library and archives to double check details in such sources as city directories. I have tried to reach current and past homeowners for their knowledge. And I have talked with many agents of Harry Norman, Realtors. Locating houses within historic neighborhoods, such as Peachtree Heights Park, has sometimes had to be by logic only, because some houses were adjacent to, but not exactly within, historic boundaries. For example, 555 Argonne Drive was built in 1913 at Arden Road when Peachtree Heights was just being planned and laid out. The brand new development did not extend that far west at that time, but we have grouped it with the other Argonne Road houses from the 1920s and 30s in Peachtree Heights.

My books: *J. Neel Reid, Architect* (1997), *Classic Atlanta* (1991), *Gardens of Georgia* (1989), and *Lewis Edmund Crook, Jr. Architect* (1984), and magazine articles, have helped with documentation. I have written as president of SAF, Inc., as a founding trustee of the Georgia Trust for Historic Preservation (1973), as a writer of architectural books, and as a native Atlantan who lives on Peachtree Street, and a ninth generation Georgian. Homeowners please accept my apology if I did not always know about all of the fine points of your improvements in a house since you took on the responsibility of making it your home. Most of these places have had numerous owners since they were built. Each owner, of course, should be recognized, if at all possible, for his and/or her contributions and tender care.

Learning is great and I have learned a good bit about these houses, even ones I have written about before, sometimes quite a few years ago. Bear in mind, however, that I am acutely aware of the differences between a house and a home. The first is a real estate and, somewhat impersonal, architectural term; the second is where one lives: raises a family, entertains, gardens, and for which one pays the taxes and fixes the roof. And sometimes even cleans the gutters and mows the lawn: greater love hath no one than that. (I prefer writing to mowing.)

William R. Mitchell Jr.
September 1999

The James Labers set an attractive pattern for those looking to enjoy the good life in Midtown: conveniently located near downtown, Piedmont Park, the Fox Theater, the Woodruff Arts Center, and other urban cultural centers.

754 Myrtle Street

The original movement into this part of the city, called Midtown since the 1970s, began in 1882 when Richard Peters built his palatial Peachtree Street mansion between Fourth and Fifth streets on a ten-acre block. (The Peters mansion stood until the 1920s, when it was replaced by the First Baptist Church.) Many of Atlanta's elite followed suit. In 1885 Richard Peters's son, Edward, built his own home, Ivy Hall (now the Mansion Restaurant), at Piedmont and Ponce de Leon avenues. The Peters Land Company owned all the land in this area, some 405 acres, where this house at 754 Myrtle Street stands.

In 1973 a lifetime resident of nearby Piedmont Avenue recalled: "This part of Atlanta was farmland not long ago. I remember hunting in back of the house. There are too many memories here, too much history. A little problem here and there in the neighborhood won't make me leave." When that was written, in fact, the neighborhood was beginning to change for the better after some bad moments in the 1940s, '50s and '60s. This house on Myrtle was part of the renewal of the Midtown Urban Conservation District sponsored by the Midtown Neighborhood Association.

The origins of the ongoing renovation of Midtown are usually traced to the architect Henri Jova's family compound on Mentelle Drive at Seventh Street, which he began in 1958. Jova is certainly one of the first urban pioneers in the area, but Joseph Blount and his architect brother, Thomas Blount, were leaders in the 1980s. Number 754 is the first house on Myrtle Street where Joe Blount lived and did some imaginative remodeling. He bought a second house, at the corner of Fifth Street to protect his original investment. Then he decided to move there because he liked the double front porches that wrap around the corner overlooking Fifth Street.

Otherwise, Joe Blount might still be living here instead of Jim and Julia Laber, 1990s urban pioneers who continue the always exciting and rewarding work of making Midtown one of Atlanta's most livable near-downtown residential communities.

Current owners: Jim and Julia Laber

This restored Ansley Park example of the Edwardian old English style intentionally reminds us of brick manor houses in the English countryside. Henry Hillyer, who had it built in 1908, and may have been his own architect, would still recognize his well-preserved handiwork.

16

229 The Prado

The Prado is named after Madrid's major avenue and museum. The name was chosen in a street-naming contest sponsored by Edwin P. Ansley as he developed Ansley Park from what had been George Washington Collier's farm. Ansley had first called the subdivision Peachtree Gardens. In 1905 he employed Solon Z. Ruff Jr., a civil engineer, to plan the neighborhood along the lines of the naturalistic and picturesque Olmsted landscape tradition that was used in Druid Hills.

The Prado is part of the earliest segment of Ansley's garden suburb. Ansley built his own home there. Number 229 The Prado was built in 1908 as the home of Henry Hillyer (d. 1926), a prominent attorney whose brother and law partner, Judge George Hillyer, was mayor of Atlanta in the 1880s. Ansley's home became the Georgia governor's mansion in 1925 and was demolished after the state built a new one in the 1960s.

It is said that Henry Hillyer designed his home himself. If so, he took as his model the sort of houses that in England were being designed a few years before by the great architect Richard Norman Shaw (1831-1912). In England the old English style was inspired by the domestic architecture of the late Tudor and early English Renaissance, especially brick manor houses. Shaw's Greenham Lodge, Berkshire, designed in 1878 and completed in 1881, is remarkably like this Atlanta Ansley Park example. If Hillyer acted as his own designer, he was certainly a talented amateur; the work of Norman Shaw as his inspiration was appropriate, since Bedford Park, London, was England's earliest garden suburb of the sort Ansley Park resembled.

During World War II, when Ansley Park's large older houses were sometimes divided into apartments, there were nine units in the main house and two in the carriage house. In the 1980s it was restored into a single-family dwelling under the direction of Atlanta architect Norman D. Askins.

Large Ansley Park houses were sometimes subdivided into apartments during the 1940s; but this house has been restored into an elegant single-family residence since the 1980s.

205 Peachtree Circle

Peachtree Circle, which makes a great arc from Peachtree Street at Fifteenth Street to Peachtree Street at Rhodes Hall, is one of Ansley Park's major, and one of the garden suburb's earliest, streets. A panoramic photograph of Peachtree Circle, taken in the first decade of Ansley Park's existence, probably in 1910, shows number 205 just at the edge of the panorama where The Prado peels off to the east. Showing in that vintage photograph is number 210 across the street, known to have been built in 1906 as the home of Dr. and Mrs. Michael Hoke. An Ansley Park prospectus from the same period shows that this was the residence of Harry Dodd.

Number 205 Peachtree Circle looks today much as it looked about 1910, a large, two-story symmetrical, almost colonial revival, post-Victorian house, with bracketed eaves and a wrap-around "semiclassical" front porch. Four doubled columnettes resting on sturdy granite piers form an open and welcoming front porch.

It took Nick and Dorothy (Dottie) Blakely O'Connor one year to renovate the house in the 1980s and make it into the home they knew it could become. Samuel Osborn was their renovation architect. The front porch and the rear of the house had to be reconstructed; they added a children's tree house and a new garage. There are nineteen rooms, many original fireplaces, and eleven-foot ceilings. Cathy Hendricks, an Ansley Park neighbor and landscape designer, redesigned the front and portions of the back garden.

The present owner, native Atlantan Douglas Candler, in 1997 purchased the house from Marshall Hahn who also had renovated the house. Candler and Craig Dick added a forty foot swimming pool in 1998, surrounded by stone terraces, rock walls and more gardens, designed by landscape architect William T. Smith. The house and its landscape setting were among the places featured on the 1999 Atlanta Botanical Garden spring tour. Candler bears a well-known Georgia surname; he is a great-great grandson of Asa Griggs Candler, one of Atlanta's landmark citizens. Founder of the Coca-Cola Company, Asa Candler was drafted by business leaders to run for the office of mayor in 1916. He won and served one term, leaving office with city finances no longer in the red, as he had promised. In this day and time that is, indeed, a legacy we can all celebrate.

Current owners: Douglas Candler and Craig Dick

Renovations over the years have preserved this home's original front symmetry, and added rear amenities. Inside, renovations and furnishings have given it a fresh aspect.

The old and the new are well-blended here where the Morgans' indoor pool and secluded rear garden merge with the main body of their home.

15 Inman Circle

Located on a landscaped hill above Inman Circle, where one turns off Peachtree Circle heading east deeper into Ansley Park, is a fine example of a renovated free classic colonial revival-style Atlanta house built in the first decade of the twentieth century. Of granite and gray shingles with white trim, it is asymmetrical, with neoclassical colonial details, freely interpreted. A "shingle-style" addition to this well renovated house provides an indoor connection to the original carriage house, now transformed into guest rooms, and also contains an indoor lap pool. It is a visually and architecturally exciting compound whether viewed from the street or under closer inspection. Old and new blend seamlessly, but with a few nice surprises, such as the indoor pool.

Neel Reid (1885-1926) designed the next-door neighboring house, on the same steep elevation, at number 17. Its Tuscan-columned portico and the Tuscan columns of the front porch here at number 15 seem neighborly indeed. Together the houses form a charming ensemble overlooking Inman Circle.

The joy of Ansley Park is the eclectic variety of homes and winding streetscape vistas set in a picturesque tree-shaded landscape, a green residential oasis near the towering concrete spires of Peachtree Street. This house seems to mirror an appealing continuum of past and future, of history and the dynamic present, that Ansley Park brings to life at every turn.

Current owners: Selene and Don Morgan

207 Fifteenth Street

Some of the first houses built in Ansley Park, soon after it was planned and laid out and lots had begun to be sold in 1904, were on Fifteenth Street. Horseless carriages were replacing earlier modes of transportation, and Ansley Park was Atlanta's first automobile suburb. Today it has become perhaps the city's most sought-after urban suburb.

A photograph from circa 1910 shows this house, the residence of F. M. Perryman, on the south side of Fifteenth Street, along with several others in Ansley Park. A pamphlet published in 1921 extolled the economics of investing in Ansley Park property, noting that George W. Collier purchased one land lot in 1847 for $150 and that his estate sold it in 1904 to Hugh T. Inman and Edwin P. Ansley for $300,000. Edwin Ansley then planned and developed Ansley Park, first called Peachtree Garden, and sold the land on one block for more than had been paid for the whole land lot!

In 1895, just a decade before Ansley Park was begun, the Cotton States and International Exposition introduced the kind of antebellum revival neoclassicism that this substantial white house at 207 Fifteenth Street represents. This classical revival manner included white-painted, many-columned "free classic" structures that were basically symmetrical and had essentially classical ornamentation, with shells, swags, and big fluted Ionic and Corinthian columns, similar to what we find here. Along Peachtree Street numerous examples of these classical revival-style mansions stood where Colony Square is today.

A preservationist couple, Nora and Gary Crawley, were responsible for the renovation of this example, one of the city's very best in that briefly fashionable style. The Crawleys recognized its value and tried to keep it true to that early twentieth-century mode. It was for them a low budget labor of love. The Crawleys were Ansley Park aficionados who supported the Ansley Park Civic Association and the Georgia Trust for Historic Preservation. Nora was an early member of the governing board of Rhodes Hall, another survivor of the first years of this historic neighborhood. Ansley Park long ago exceeded the dreams of its original investors and developers because of such people.

Current owners: Mr. and Mrs. William A. Lobb II

Ansley Park is an "urban suburb" in the heart of Midtown; secluded gardens have skyscrapers as backdrops.

38 Peachtree Circle

Many Atlanta homes, far too many, had a connection with the tragic Air France crash at Orly Airport in Paris on June 3, 1962, in which 106 Atlanta Art Association patrons lost their lives. Mrs. William Richardson, at that time the owner of 38 Peachtree Circle, was one of those on the Art Association tour of European art centers. This great loss of life became the catalyst, of course, for building the Memorial (Woodruff) Arts Center on Peachtree Street, on the edge of Ansley Park, near this house. And although Mrs. Richardson did not return home, and her house had to be sold, it eventually fell into other good hands.

The process of a speculative renovation had begun when Mr. and Mrs. Moreland G. Smith purchased it in the fall of 1965 to renovate as their home. In May of the following year they moved in after Moreland Smith (1906-89), a talented and experienced professional architect, renovated it extensively inside and out for himself and his wife, Marjorie Levy Smith. The Smiths removed to Atlanta from Montgomery, Alabama, where he had been a founder of the firm of Sherlock, Smith and Adams, Architects and Engineers.

Today Moreland Smith's elegant renovation is still very much as he designed it in 1965-66. It is a great credit to Ansley Park as it has continued to evolve since the neighborhood's inception as Atlanta's first automobile suburb in the first decade of the twentieth century. Subsequent owners have recognized the beauty and appropriateness of the Smiths' renovation, and this house, in the thirty-odd years since its completion – if indeed, the renovation of any Ansley Park house is ever exactly complete – has become a model of taste and elegance along historic Peachtree Circle. We believe Mrs. Richardson would approve of what has happened to number 38.

Current owners: Wit and Donna Hall

106 Inman Circle

Built in 1911 as the home of J. H. Ewing, a noted Atlanta Realtor, this is another Ansley Park example of an antebellum neoclassical revival house from the early days of Edwin Ansley's garden suburb. (Compare it with number 207 Fifteenth Street.) This example is even more directly derived from the style of some of the buildings put up for the Cotton States and International Exposition held in 1895 at the site where Piedmont Park is today. The wide band of intricate carvings, edged with denticulation, that forms an architrave above the simple Tuscan columns is a distinguishing feature tying this house to the architecture of that World's Fair-like exposition.

Four stone chimneys and a four-columned, two-level portico resting on a sturdy granite podium anchor this revival of antebellum architecture commanding the hill above Inman Circle. The recently installed landscape scheme, with its intricately patterned lawn and evergreen plantings, complements the fresh new yellow and white coloring of yet another one of Ansley Park's many and diverse dowager mansions with a new lease on life. Investments in the future of historic Ansley Park by young new owners, such as David York and John Hogg, assure its continued desirability as one of the city's oldest garden suburbs.

Current owners: Dr. John Hogg and Mr. David York

This front-yard garden is both traditional and original, a fresh setting for a mature, neoclassical house that has been handsomely renovated.

41 Palisades Road

Brookwood Hills may well be the beginning of the Buckhead suburbs. At Palisades Road, N.E., the street signs change from Peachtree Street to Peachtree Road. The name Brookwood dates back to the 1880s when there were country estates along Peachtree, one called Brookwood.

Brookwood Hills is a well-defined residential area on the east side of Peachtree with limited access at Huntington, Palisades, and Brighton roads. Developers Benjamin F. Burdett and his son assembled sixty-five acres between 1912 and 1922. The civil engineer O. F. Kauffman planned the naturalistic layout according to the ideas of Frederick Law Olmsted.

Brookwood Hills was designed for upper middle-class automobile owners and is still considered one of Atlanta's most desirable intown garden suburbs. It is convenient and beautifully green and wooded with elegant, traditional two-story residences, most dating from the 1920s and 1930s.

Number 41 Palisades is a perfect example of the values of this tight-knit community in preserving what is best about the place. The current owners, Mr. and Mrs. Douglas S. Holladay Jr., moved to this area of Atlanta from Virginia in 1992. When the house came on the market in 1994, they were the first to see it, and they signed a contract to buy it from the Hillyer Youngs that day. Larré Holladay was charmed by its wonderful condition and Mediterranean style, its "airy openness, yet sturdiness."

Rebecca and Hillyer Young had renovated the 1920s house with the help of two talented Atlantans, architect Kemp Mooney and decorator Nancy Braithwaite. The Youngs had Mooney preserve its original character, as viewed from the street, the garden, and inside. The exterior stucco, repaired by Rumanian workers, was matched with interior stucco, an idea of the contractor, Franz Schneider. A new semi-hexagonal tower with a breakfast room surrounded by French doors on the garden side looks like part of the old house. Tile floors enhance the Mediterranean style, as does the wisteria-draped pergola in the spirit of ancient Pompeii. This classic Brookwood Hills home has helped make the Holladays happy that his work brought them from Richmond to Atlanta.

Current owners: Mr. and Mrs. Douglas S. Holladay Jr.

Larré and Douglas Holladay were drawn to this Brookwood Hills villa because of the blend of sturdiness and openness, represented by the garden elevation above.

31

2287 Dellwood Drive

The colonial revival style of the early twentieth century produced wonderfully livable and attractive houses that seem like home. Haynes Manor, off Peachtree Battle Avenue, has numerous appealing examples of colonial revival. Built on a corner lot at Woodward Way in 1937 by John R. Pattillo, this two-story frame representative is an exemplary model of the style. For many years it was the home of the John Woodalls and now of Beth and Jeff Ervin. Beth is an interior decorator who appreciates its good lines and has improved upon them with the help of Jack Davis, her architect and friend. Davis and Ervin redesigned the arched entry porch, adding trelliswork, a favored revival detail, which is so appropriate that it seems part of the original 1937 conception. Another of Beth's projects is to make the garage into a guest house that will seem to have been there all along. Years from now the Ervins' improvements will seem all of a piece with the original design (and some future owner will bless them for the new kitchen and bathrooms). The colonial revival continues to be revived as new generations discover its "down-home" charms.

Current owners: Beth and Jeff Ervin

365 Peachtree Battle Avenue

This is one of the earliest of the manor houses of Haynes Manor, and it is sited on the highest ground in the neighborhood, affording a view of the downtown skyline. It is diagonally across the street from Eugene W. Haynes's own home that he built as a model for the residential area he began to develop in 1926 west of Peachtree Heights Park, which he called Haynes Manor. The subdivision continued from here toward Northside Drive and ran north and south of Peachtree Battle Avenue, which was extended by name but not with the unusually wide median-divided roadway. The Peachtree Heights part of the avenue was planned by the architects Carrere & Hastings from 1911 to 1915 for E. Rivers Realty Company's Peachtree Heights.

Eugene Haynes was a well-known jeweler who became a real estate developer. Some of the streets in his development, going west, are Dellwood, Haven Ridge, Montview, Alton, and Manor Ridge. In this area the Civil War Battle of Peachtree Creek occurred on July 20, 1864, giving the name Peachtree Battle Avenue to the main road from Peachtree Road west to Northside Drive. Federal troops came through here from the north to attack the Confederate lines at Collier Road.

This Mediterranean manor, built in 1926-27, commands the high ground above Peachtree Battle Avenue as though this were "General" Haynes's headquarters. Haynes probably built it for sale, and the first owner was A.R. Cannon, who lived here until 1932. It is a perfectly balanced two-story stucco and tile-roofed Spanish Renaissance revival fantasy of the sort Addison Mizner introduced for the very rich of Palm Beach, Florida, during the boom years after World War I. The matching balconies with French doors are especially romantic details, as are the balancing porch wings, with small baroque columns supporting arch motifs. Altogether these features complete the symmetrical rhythm of the inviting façade. The Dennis Zakases, who liked its location, site and style, became the owners in June, 1996, adding a rear wing designed for them by architect Norris Broyles III to blend with the existing architecture.

Current owners: Dennis and Martie Zakas

Because of history, this quiet civilized street, with comfortable homes and peaceful parterre gardens, is named after a battle, but there is charm in the contrast.

314 Peachtree Battle Avenue

As Peachtree Heights Park becomes Haynes Manor at Dellwood Drive, on Peachtree Battle Avenue at the southeast corner is an early 1930s Tudor cottage. Its two-story, steeply pitched front-facing gable, rock-clad entry porch, and stucco walls are all typical of this eclectic, period revival style, which was as fashionable in the 1920s and '30s as the colonial revival. It is still much sought after.

Number 314 Peachtree Battle is such a fine example of this sixteenth-century English vernacular house type that it was featured among six residences on the Atlanta Preservation Center's 1997 Peachtree Battle Tour of Homes. Randi and Syd Williams were the homeowners then, and are now. Even though it was remodeled in the mid-1970s and in 1995, its 1930s period charm has only been enhanced. The house and its garden setting relate hand-in-glove, and there is a cozy sense of privacy and comfort that the old English word *home* brings to mind: familiar ground, a congenial environment, a family gathering place.

Current owners: Randi and Syd Williams

353 Peachtree Battle Avenue

Most of the homes in Haynes Manor, which begins with this house at the northwest corner of Peachtree Battle Avenue and Dellwood Drive, reflect the neighborhood's name: manor houses in one of the traditional period styles, with brick, stone, and stucco exteriors. Inside are high ceilings, real plaster walls, moldings, hardwood floors, and spacious rooms. Most properties average a half-acre; some are larger. This one is one-and-a-half acres. All have large shade trees, broad lawns, and landscaped garden settings. Eugene V. Haynes lived at number 426, diagonally across the street from number 353, in a model of 1920s Mediterranean/Spanish eclecticism.

For many years, number 353 was the home of the Lorenz Neuhoffs. Later Dr. and Mrs. Alton V. Hallum raised their family here; he was an outstanding eye doctor. Constructed in 1927-28 on a high ridge above the street, it was one of the first houses that Eugene Haynes built for sale in his development, and it is one of the largest Tudor revival manors in the neighborhood. This style was based on a variety of late Medieval English precedents, freely mixed: steeply pitched roofs, parapeted gables, massive chimneys, and Tudor arches (a sort of "flat-pointed" arch). The current owner purchased it in 1992 and has since added a swimming pool.

In April 1926, when this house was about to be constructed, an Atlanta architect, G. Lloyd Preacher, who designed many houses similar to this one, especially in Druid Hills where he lived on Ponce de Leon Avenue, wrote in the *City Builder*: "A prominent official of a mid-western city was being driven through the residential districts of Atlanta a few months ago. As he proceeded through Druid Hills and Ansley Park to the outer Peachtree section, he said to his host: 'Atlanta has a greater proportion of beautiful homes than any other city of which I have knowledge. It must be an unending delight to live in such surroundings.'"

The delight continues as we end this century and begin anew.

Current owner: Mr. K. Hernandez

The tender loving care of successive owners and the new amenities such as an elegant swimming pool, combine to create a growing and evolving beauty in Haynes Manor since its inception in the 1920s.

Dan Carithers's own home suggests what he achieves for others with his interior designs. Clearly, he enjoys his work, and we are fortunate to catch a glimpse of his mastery of decorating for Nancy and himself.

2499 Montview Drive

As the Haynes Manor neighborhood began to grow, William C. Dumas, a manufacturing chemist, built this house in 1937 at the corner of Montview and Manor Ridge drives. Well designed to suit that corner location, this is an eclectic period house reminiscent of colonial Pennsylvania with a *soupçon* of France in the dormers. The walkway to the front doorway comes from Montview, and the driveway to the garage and rear garden is on Manor Ridge.

For twenty-two years, this has been the home of Dan Carithers. Carithers is one of Atlanta's favorite interior decorators and designers; naturally, his own home is stylish and comfortable. He and his wife, Nancy, love the convenient location only blocks from Peachtree Road. Carithers has lived in the neighborhood for most of his adult life. Haynes Manor is home.

Dan Carithers has decorated houses for many fashionable people. In the May-June 1999 issue of *Southern Accents*, Carithers is described as "one of the country's interior design luminaries"; in that regard, among his credits, he was a design consultant for Baker Furniture for many years.

Number 2499 Montview Drive reflects his understanding and mastery of classic taste in the decorative arts. The *savoir faire* of Dan Carithers's refined sense of beauty must be a great pleasure to experience daily as we glimpse here in these views of his own Buckhead home. As Carithers said, "No room has been left untouched."

Current owners: Nancy and Dan Carithers

When early twentieth-century designers discovered the French door, life in suburban houses blossomed: the inside and the outside could be merged into harmonious light-filled spaces. Period houses such as this could be given fresh new interpretations.

315 Peachtree Battle Avenue
Bellemonde

Peachtree Battle Avenue from Peachtree Road to Dellwood Drive was part of the original Peachtree Heights Park planned in 1910 and 1911, then revised in 1915 and 1925. Where the wide median park ends in front of this house, at the corner of Dellwood, is the beginning of Haynes Manor, which Eugene V. Haynes began in 1926. Number 315 Peachtree Battle was built in 1929 for Hiram Wesley Evans of Texas, who moved to Atlanta to become Imperial Wizard of the Ku Klux Klan, a position he held until 1939. In 1935 Evans built another house across the street, at 306 Peachtree Battle, in the art deco style with an intricately detailed limestone facade. He sold his Georgian revival redbrick house to Raymond A. Kline, a Macy's executive who moved to Atlanta to be general manager of the Davison-Paxon department store in downtown Atlanta.

Marbury and Cathy Rainer, who moved here in 1987, are considered the fourth owners of this fascinating landmark. Civic spirited, the Rainers have generously shared their home with the world: in 1997 their terraced gardens were included on the Atlanta Botanical Garden tour in the spring and, in the fall, the Atlanta Preservation Center Tour of Homes.

Theirs is that rare private home in Atlanta that is still unaltered since it was built. Two of the mementos of Imperial Wizard Hiram Evans's tenure are in the study. A large fireplace is surrounded by a granite mantel with a keystone bearing an inscription that could be cryptic if we didn't know the story: "From top of Stone Mountain." That's where the KKK once held their rallies. Also, in back of a concealed closet there is a huge safe believed to be original to the wizard's era.

By contrast, however, the first floor of the house opens through numerous arched French doors onto terraces and gardens. The home was used in 1991 as the set for the television movie, *White Lie*. You cannot be less secretive than that.

Current owners: Marbury and Kathy Rainer

7 Vernon Road

This Regency villa started life in 1939. Francis Abreu of Abreu & Robeson, Architects, designed it as the home of Oliver M. Healey. At that time Vernon Road had been paved for only a few years. Next door, to the north, was the home of Healey's brother, William. The Healey family had been in Atlanta since the nineteenth century. Abreu had come to Sea Island, Georgia, as that resort was developed, designing some of the earliest cottages for the Sea Island Company, and then to Atlanta.

Today 7 Vernon Road is a larger house, renovated and enlarged in the spirit of Abreu's late 1930s Regency revival style. The architect for the current work, John (Jack) Davis, worked with Dr. and Mrs. Carl R. Hartrampf Jr. to bring out and add to the best aspects of Abreu's original structure.

There had been a vogue for Regency during the depression; it was a stylish yet simplified and understated (slightly modern) form of neoclassicism, with its plain stucco surfaces and contrasting, decorative iron work. The classical orders were not as much in evidence as with the earlier Georgian periods, instead only implied in the scale and proportions. Also, windows were large, rendering exterior walls more transparent and interiors more light filled.

Davis and the Hartrampfs have given the Healey's villa a Palladian five-part plan, faced in stucco to blend with the main block of the mansion. Landscape architecture was by the husband and wife team Mary Palmer and Hugh Dargan. Evidently, it was they who added to the overall symmetry of effect by making a new driveway from Vernon Road on axis with the front doorway.

The Hartrampf's furnishings and improvements complement the Regency architecture of their Buckhead villa. Among the special decorative aspects of their home that should be mentioned is a collection of prints and engravings that their son-in-law, W. Graham Arader III, has helped them assemble.

Current owners: Dr. and Mrs. Carl R. Hartrampf

Add to the original building date that of the current work that has made the Healey's Regency villa the Hartrampf's.

220 West Andrews Drive

In this writer's library is a book that belonged to the architect of this house. The book is Lewis Crook's copy of *Domestic Gothic of the Tudor Period*, published in 1927, the year before Crook designed this Tudor Gothic revival house for Percy R. Baker; it was Ivey & Crook job number 211.

Buck Crook was a versatile, eclectic designer, a beaux arts traditionalist who graduated first in his class from the Georgia Tech School of Architecture. He became a Neel Reid protégé and employee and then went into practice in 1923 with another Reid associate, Ed Ivey. The firm of Ivey & Crook was prolific, building hundreds of houses (and other structures) expertly sited, designed, supervised, and landscaped. Crook's 1927 color rendering of a house for Dr. Newton Craig, built at 347 West Muscogee Avenue, only blocks from this house on West Andrews Drive, reveals Buck Crook's mastery of the style of brick, stucco, and half-timbered English houses of the late Middle Ages, creatively adapted in the twentieth century.

West Andrews Drive winds between West Paces Ferry Road and Habersham Road in Peachtree Heights Park. It is the location of many handsome period houses such as this; they continue to make comfortable traditional homes, with more than a hint of history, as they are remodeled and enlarged to meet present-day expectations. The architect in charge of remodeling this one was Norman Askins, one of Crook's fellow Georgia Tech-trained architects. (Crook was class of 1919, when historic architecture was a vital part of the curriculum; Askins was 1966, when modernism was the rule, but he sought graduate study at the University of Virginia.) Askins is as adept as his beaux arts predecessors were, although traditional eclecticism is not the trend among most of his professional colleagues. A house such as this proves that more of them should study the historic styles for use in our day, as the architecture schools once taught.

Current owners: Mr. and Mrs. Thomas M. Holder

Remodeling a period house of the 1920s requires taste and skill to add 1990s state-of-the-art fittings so that they seem at home. For the owners, a newly designed kitchen is a welcome addition to any older home.

2893 Andrews Drive

This house was "built to order for Strother Fleming Sr. by Frazier & Bodin, Architects, in spring 1924," said Mrs. William M. (Dorothy Dean) Mason. "I can tell you this because I have a copy of the blueprints that came with the house when I inherited it from my mother." Mrs. Mason's parents purchased this place from the Flemings in the spring of 1934. Their real estate agent was Mrs. Harry Norman Sr.

Dorothy Mason's mother lived here until her death in 1978, at which time the homeplace became Mrs. Mason's. She took possession six months later, in early 1979, living here comfortably and steadfastly ever after.

Frazier & Bodin did most of their domestic architecture in Tuxedo Park, northwest of here. This is a rare example of their work in Peachtree Heights Park, as the pace of development began to pick up in the prosperous 1920s. The appealing solid geometry of this two-story brick beaux arts colonial revival-style family home depends on its satisfying symmetry and such details as the arched transom and sidelights of leaded glass with a small-scaled classical portico and the three perfect pedimented dormers rising from the low-pitched gray roof. Arched Renaissance cornucopia decorations above four ground-floor sash windows and the handsomely detailed fleur-de-lis pattern of the wrought-iron balusters of a gracefully curving staircase say again that it was designed by architects trained in the beaux arts tradition and built in 1924, rather than a century earlier.

In fast-paced Atlanta, that only two families have called 2893 Andrews home adds to the ambience of history that Mrs. Mason's residence quietly and privately projects from its screened site.

Current owner: Mrs. William M. Mason

Mrs. William M. Mason has carefully maintained the home's original design and character.

3414 Habersham Road

This twentieth-century, Regency-style brick house has grown in size, while retaining its original architectural character, since it was built in 1937 by Wayne and Lydia Martin. The Martins' daughter, Matilda Martin Dobbs, lived here as a child; she recalled that Tucker & Howell designed it, but the use of old whitewashed bricks was her mother's idea. So that they could move closer to Peachtree Road and Matilda's school, her parents sold it in 1942, during wartime, to Joe High Williams. Later it became the home of Jere M. Mills, who had a swimming pool installed.

Next came Norman Powell Pendley and his wife, Lavania; Pendley was president of W. E. Browne Decorating Company, a decorative arts authority and porcelain expert. For generations, Browne Decorating was an Atlanta institution, but it closed in the mid-1990s. Norman Pendley lived here in the 1980s, until he died. His death ended an era in Atlanta and hastened the demise of the highly respected old decorating firm.

Atlanta landscape architect Edward L. Daugherty designed the walled courtyard after Mr. Pendley's death. The courtyard was part of a project, directed by the architecture firm of Norman Askins, to increase the size of the house. There are about one-and-a-quarter acres at 3414 Habersham Road in this Tuxedo Park/Valley Road "suburban-urban" townhouse worthy of Bath, England, the home of the Regency style.

Current owners: Mr. and Mrs. John Wigodsky

This Regency-style house designed in 1937 by Tucker & Howell has continued to expand seamlessly according to the original taste, so that today it is a handsome and harmonious whitewashed brick manor perhaps twice as large as when it was built.

53

3164 Habersham Road

This part of Habersham Road from Argonne Drive to West Paces Ferry Road is the seamless extension of the original road laid out as part of Peachtree Heights Park. Number 3164 Habersham dates from 1933. It was built for Mr. and Mrs. Frederick W. Patterson. Fred Patterson (1893-1972) was an Atlanta native who became a partner in his father's funeral home business, H. W. Patterson & Son, in 1924; he was also founder of a life insurance company.

His architects were the firm of Hentz, Adler & Shutze (which also designed the Spring Hill Mortuary for the Pattersons in 1927-28.) Based on eighteenth-century New England farmhouse precedents, the Patterson house sits on a hill on the west side of Habersham. In 1940 it was included on the Egleston Hospital Spring Tour of Homes, and soon thereafter the Pattersons moved to an enlarged version of this same house, also designed by Philip Shutze, on Northside Drive (now the home of Mr. and Mrs. Julian S. Carr).

The same arched porch with trelliswork is a graceful motif on both versions of these Patterson houses. This Habersham Road version also combines frame and bricks and an informal, vernacular layout; it is turned on the lot in such a way that the main entrance is on the side of the house away from the street, providing visual surprise and privacy, and it uses the deep lot to an advantage.

Later, in 1951, Fred Patterson had yet another home built for himself in the Buckhead area not far from here. This time the architects were Ivey & Crook; it stands at 2959 Andrews Drive. (See page 82 of this book.)

The current owners, Dr. and Mrs. Robert W. Powers Jr., bought the house from the estate of Oscar G. Davis Jr. in 1990. They purchased it because of its history, beauty, and convenient location. Daily it becomes their family's homeplace as it draws nearer to being seventy years old.

Current owners: Dr. and Mrs. Robert W. Powers Jr.

10 West Andrews Drive

West Andrews Drive meanders from Habersham Road to West Paces Ferry north of Peachtree Heights Park. The neighborhood attracts nice, quiet families. The lots are large, as are the houses – most of which date from the 1920s and '30s. This one, on a hill at number 10 West Andrews, dates from 1925-26. It was built as the residence of Frank G. North, a textile manufacturer, who lived here until the 1940s. The style is "tile-roof Mediterranean villa," similar to many houses built at the same time on Springdale and Oakdale roads, in the Druid Hills suburb of Atlanta.

Druid Hills, in fact, set the standard for this type of picturesque, heavily forested neighborhood, where vegetated hills and dales provide interesting building sites and wooded neighborhood parks. The houses had sleeping porches, high ceilings, thick walls, many windows, French doors, wide lawns, and deep garden settings. There is some visual diversity in the whole ensemble, but mostly a sense of harmony, house to house and street by street.

Perhaps it is no coincidence that the current owner of this comfortable Buckhead house is a descendant of one of the main developers of Druid Hills, Asa Griggs Candler. The Very Reverend Samuel Candler, dean of the nearby Episcopal Cathedral of Saint Philip, purchased this house two years ago, partly because of its proximity to the cathedral where he officiates. Also, he and his wife and children needed a spacious home for the sort of receiving a man of the cloth often must do. The Candlers moved here after architect Norman D. Askins modified and enlarged it for a developer to sell. Then, Spitzmiller & Norris, traditionalist architects, renovated and enlarged it for the Candlers to suit their needs.

Even so, the prospect of the house that one sees from West Andrews is a comfortable Atlanta home of the *Driving Miss Daisy* vintage, between the world wars. Inside, a quiet charm prevails. One feels that musical harmonies might momentarily emanate from some of Dean Candler's fine collection of antique musical instruments.

Current owners: The Very Reverend and Mrs. Samuel G. Candler

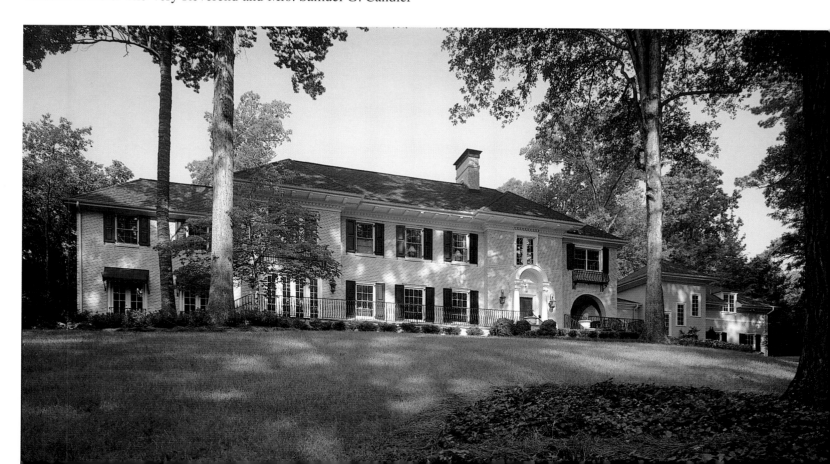

2888 Habersham Road

Mrs. Trammell Scott seems to have been the first resident of this handsomely and deceptively simple classical Habersham Road house. The design has long been attributed to Neel Reid (1885-1926). Prof. James Grady (1907-92), in *Architecture of Neel Reid in Georgia*, published in 1973 by the Peachtree-Cherokee Garden Club Trust, calls it a house "for T. W. Watson," dating it 1921. The owners when Grady wrote were Mr. and Mrs. Joseph Miller, who bought it in 1965. The present owners are Mr. and Mrs. Richard Lee, whose home it became in 1997 because of its beauty and location. They hope it will prove to be by Reid, although there are no surviving drawings or blueprints among the thousands for Hentz, Reid & Adler that are housed at the Atlanta Historical Society.

The 1928 *Atlanta City Directory* first shows a residence at 2888 Habersham Road; the resident is Trammell Scott. There is nothing listed there in 1926, the year of Reid's death, or in 1927. No Watson is listed among later owners.

This writer's *J. Neel Reid, Architect of Hentz, Reid & Adler*, published in 1997, has an annotated list of Reid commissions based on the firm's own jobs list. For this work, he studied and researched all extant drawings and consulted scores of other sources, including the garden club's research guides for its 1973 book. The only job the firm did for a client named Watson was for Mrs. O. G. Watson, number 499, in 1922, but no drawings survived if, indeed, the commission ever reached the drawing stage.

Could Mrs. O. G. Watson have married Trammell Scott and then built the house after Reid died? One of the associates in the firm, who became a partner after Reid's death, was Philip Trammell Shutze. Could Trammell Scott have been a relative of his? Could this be a Philip Shutze design in the Reid manner from about 1927-28? Did Mrs. Scott always just attribute it to Neel Reid after his firm became Hentz, Adler and Shutze?

Habersham Road in Peachtree Heights was "Neel Reid Country." Stylistically the scale and proportion of the casual classicism of 2888 Habersham undoubtedly belong among this master's many works in that neighborhood. Professor Grady thought so and wrote, "This design is an example of Reid's ability to give distinction with the simplest means."

Current owners: Mr. and Mrs. Richard H. Lee

59

2905 Andrews Drive

Few could imagine today that such an appealing residence, a charming Andrews Drive home, could have begun life in 1931 as a "garage apartment." The main house was never built, but that is not easily detected because of the beauty of the house that stands there now.

The apartment, however, was enlarged several times and a garage enclosed for more living space prior to the 1986-87 renovation by the former owners, Tate and Constance Wright, who acted as their own architects on the project. The size of the existing structure was doubled and the exterior of the house was the Wright's interpretation of the colonial revival. The Wrights were inspired by the work and taste of architects Neel Reid and Philip Shutze, and helped by an "artist-carpenter" James Coombs.

Attracted to its spacious layout and easy flow, Doug and Carey Benham purchased the residence in January 1998. Carey, who is an art consultant and decorator, completely redesigned the interior of the house. In conjunction with Atlanta artists, Brian Carter and Greg Little, bold colors were used to accentuate the couple's treasured art collection. Rooms combine a touch of formality, with a warm and inviting spirit of comfort.

As a home for entertaining large groups as well as small, intimate gatherings, the Benham residence is a proud member of the Peachtree Heights Park community. When it was included on the Atlanta Preservation Center's tour of the neighborhood in October 1994, people were surprised to learn about its history, which only grows in interest with the years since its modest beginnings in the 1930s.

Current owners: Doug and Carey Benham

The current owners of this classic Buckhead landmark are interested in its history, while adding new chapters. The previous owners have shared with the Dubrofs that the estate was once called *The Spring House* because of a spring on the property popular in the neighborhood.

220 West Andrews Drive

In this writer's library is a book that belonged to the architect of this house. The book is Lewis Crook's copy of *Domestic Gothic of the Tudor Period*, published in 1927, the year before Crook designed this Tudor Gothic revival house for Percy R. Baker; it was Ivey & Crook job number 211.

Buck Crook was a versatile, eclectic designer, a beaux arts traditionalist who graduated first in his class from the Georgia Tech School of Architecture. He became a Neel Reid protégé and employee and then went into practice in 1923 with another Reid associate, Ed Ivey. The firm of Ivey & Crook was prolific, building hundreds of houses (and other structures) expertly sited, designed, supervised, and landscaped. Crook's 1927 color rendering of a house for Dr. Newton Craig, built at 347 West Muscogee Avenue, only blocks from this house on West Andrews Drive, reveals Buck Crook's mastery of the style of brick, stucco, and half-timbered English houses of the late Middle Ages, creatively adapted in the twentieth century.

West Andrews Drive winds between West Paces Ferry Road and Habersham Road in Peachtree Heights Park. It is the location of many handsome period houses such as this; they continue to make comfortable traditional homes, with more than a hint of history, as they are remodeled and enlarged to meet present-day expectations. The architect in charge of remodeling this one was Norman Askins, one of Crook's fellow Georgia Tech-trained architects. (Crook was class of 1919, when historic architecture was a vital part of the curriculum; Askins was 1966, when modernism was the rule, but he sought graduate study at the University of Virginia.) Askins is as adept as his beaux arts predecessors were, although traditional eclecticism is not the trend among most of his professional colleagues. A house such as this proves that more of them should study the historic styles for use in our day, as the architecture schools once taught.

Current owners: Mr. and Mrs. Thomas M. Holder

Remodeling a period house of the 1920s requires taste and skill to add 1990s state-of-the-art fittings so that they seem at home. For the owners, a newly designed kitchen is a welcome addition to any older home.

2893 Andrews Drive

This house was "built to order for Strother Fleming Sr. by Frazier & Bodin, Architects, in spring 1924," said Mrs. William M. (Dorothy Dean) Mason. "I can tell you this because I have a copy of the blueprints that came with the house when I inherited it from my mother." Mrs. Mason's parents purchased this place from the Flemings in the spring of 1934. Their real estate agent was Mrs. Harry Norman Sr.

Dorothy Mason's mother lived here until her death in 1978, at which time the homeplace became Mrs. Mason's. She took possession six months later, in early 1979, living here comfortably and steadfastly ever after.

Frazier & Bodin did most of their domestic architecture in Tuxedo Park, northwest of here. This is a rare example of their work in Peachtree Heights Park, as the pace of development began to pick up in the prosperous 1920s. The appealing solid geometry of this two-story brick beaux arts colonial revival-style family home depends on its satisfying symmetry and such details as the arched transom and sidelights of leaded glass with a small-scaled classical portico and the three perfect pedimented dormers rising from the low-pitched gray roof. Arched Renaissance cornucopia decorations above four ground-floor sash windows and the handsomely detailed fleur-de-lis pattern of the wrought-iron balusters of a gracefully curving staircase say again that it was designed by architects trained in the beaux arts tradition and built in 1924, rather than a century earlier.

In fast-paced Atlanta, that only two families have called 2893 Andrews home adds to the ambience of history that Mrs. Mason's residence quietly and privately projects from its screened site.

Current owner: Mrs. William M. Mason

Mrs. William M. Mason has carefully maintained the home's original design and character.

2789 Habersham Road

Until 1997 this house was 2 Vernon Road, and its name was Lane's End. It was reached straight down a 350-foot-long carriage drive from Vernon Road. Originally the property went from this almost hidden entrance on Vernon Road through to Habersham Road, the parcel seeming even more extensive because it is adjacent to Sibley Park at the corner of Habersham and West Wesley roads. William Pauley, one of Atlanta's best landscape architects when Lane's End was completed in 1924-25, helped Neel Reid plan these extensive grounds. Pauley's renderings of the landscape plan are illustrated in *Garden History of Georgia* (1933).

This was Hentz, Reid & Adler job number 527, designed in 1923-24. The garden side of this Atlanta version of a Maryland manor is visible from Habersham Road; its neoclassical portico affords porch-sitters one of Atlanta's most breathtakingly beautiful landscape prospects.

The original owner sold the place in the mid-1930s to the Carlyle Frasers, and the Fraser estate sold the property to Mr. and Mrs. Jerry Dubrof in 1996. The Dubrofs have kept the Habersham Road façade as Reid designed it. They have brought a curving driveway from Habersham Road through the north woods to the Vernon Road entrance and added a colonnade, garages and other additions inspired by details on Reid's original southern Palladian five-part plan. Reid's arched semi-hexagonal entrance porch in the Tuscan order, with a sheaf of wheat balustrade, still reposes exactly as he designed it for the east entrance elevation of Lane's End. Reid based this porch on one at Gunston Hall in Fairfax County, Virginia.

Peachtree Heights Park was "Neel Reid country." There were seventeen Hentz, Reid & Adler domestic designs in Peachtree Heights from 1914 through 1926. Reid's houses were created for specific sites and set in gardens, front, sides, and rear. There were six Neel Reids on Habersham (now seven with Lane's End's new address), five on Andrews, three on Cherokee, and two on West Wesley. The romantically classical garden façade of Lane's End is one of the best known of these Reid landmarks, with all good reason.

Current owners: Mr. and Mrs. Jerry Dubrof

430 Argonne Drive

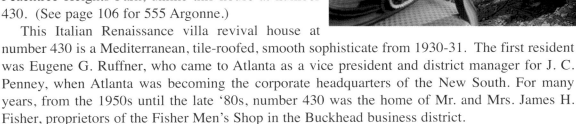

Argonne Drive is a long, quiet, wooded street, winding through changing elevations that create interesting building sites. An eclectic collection of house styles beginning in the early 1930s has evolved. One house, where the street meets Arden Road at number 555, is the street's oldest. When it was first built it was probably not originally part of Argonne Drive at all, but a country house at Arden Road, and not part of Peachtree Heights Park, unlike this house at number 430. (See page 106 for 555 Argonne.)

This Italian Renaissance villa revival house at number 430 is a Mediterranean, tile-roofed, smooth sophisticate from 1930-31. The first resident was Eugene G. Ruffner, who came to Atlanta as a vice president and district manager for J. C. Penney, when Atlanta was becoming the corporate headquarters of the New South. For many years, from the 1950s until the late '80s, number 430 was the home of Mr. and Mrs. James H. Fisher, proprietors of the Fisher Men's Shop in the Buckhead business district.

The owners since 1989 are Alfred D. Kennedy, a founder and executive director of the Atlanta Opera Company, and Dr. William R. Kenny, director of respiratory care at Piedmont Hospital. (Kennedy's grandfather's house was 2868 Andrews Drive, on pages 92-93.) Grand opera runs in that family. Alfred Kennedy's father, who died in 1983, was the longtime president of the Atlanta Music Festival Association, the organization once responsible for bringing the Metropolitan Opera to Atlanta during a now-discontinued annual spring season.

Today the Atlanta Opera Company has revived the long tradition of opera in Atlanta dating back to the turn of the century. As the home of Atlanta's opera impresario, this Italianate villa should be comfortable with, and not at all surprised to have, the great melodies of Puccini and Verdi sung by great voices and rattling its handsome Mediterranean clay-tile roof.

Current owners: Mr. Alfred D. Kennedy and Dr. William R. Kenny

7 Habersham Way

Habersham Way is a quiet byway winding between Andrews Drive and Habersham Road in the heart of Peachtree Heights Park. The oldest house on the street, at number 10, is Mayfair, the large old 1920s estate at the middle bend, behind a white-painted brick wall. Across the street, at number 5, is a charming brick house designed by Brevard S. Williams of Brevard Interiors, which once stood on Peachtree Street in downtown Atlanta. Williams built a Norman French *manoir*, as his own home. The house next door, also of brick with half-timbering and other authentic provincial details, was designed in 1935 for the Channing Whitmans by architect James Wise. Together, these houses seem to be a fresh breath of medieval air in the midst of houses built in other styles.

One of the glories of number 7 Habersham Way is, in fact, a feature that must be experienced first hand, since it is not on view from the street: the unique rear quarry garden, three hundred feet back, where on a hot summer's day the temperature is degrees cooler. There a small spring-fed waterfall tumbles down into a pool from the cliffs of the gray granite walls, said to be the remnants of a Confederate-era rock quarry. The brook meanders through the back garden of native plants along its banks, with ferns, woodland flowers, and mosses making a secret, mountain-like garden in the very heart of residential Buckhead.

The front country garden bordered with a fence of old chestnut features boxwood parterres and a rose garden that passersby can enjoy: it is one of the neighborhood amenities that make Habersham Way such an appealing discovery. Both the front and rear gardens reflect the taste and work of the current owners who made it their home in 1989 after six months of renovation, inside and out.

No wonder Habersham Way is a popular destination for home owners. This garden was one of seven presented on the ninth annual Gardens for Connoisseurs Tour, May 9-10, 1992. At that time, the current owners, Dr. and Mrs. Herndon Murray, had been home here long enough to welcome other gardeners ("the yards are why we moved here"); they happily remain to welcome us now.

Current owners: Dr. and Mrs. H. Herndon Murray

The James Christians have furnished their home in an exciting, eclectic manner that highlights traditionalism with contrast.

2 Habersham Park

Architect Norman Davenport Askins, a native of the garden suburb Mountain Brook, home of the finest traditional domestic architecture in Birmingham, was commissioned to design this house in the mid-1970s. Askins is, perhaps, the classical revivalist of tradition-minded Buckhead, where he settled after earning his B.A. in architecture at Georgia Tech in 1966 and two years later his master's degree in architectural history from the University of Virginia. Askins could well be described as a present-day follower of America's great neoclassicist Thomas Jefferson, founder and designer of that university.

Askins was asked to design a "model home" for Habersham Park, a development on part of the estate originally called Mayfair. He designed four houses for this small, enclave neighborhood just off Habersham Way.

Mayfair, a large estate almost hidden in the bend of Habersham Way is a romantically beautiful evocation of white-columned, antebellum Georgia. Some of the acreage from the original estate became Habersham Park. Norman Askins made number 2 an understated story-and-a-half southern colonial-style shingled cottage, as though it were an estate house at Mayfair. Absolutely symmetrical and modestly scaled, its aura of Jeffersonian classicism is appropriate for the designer's training and its site on the edge of the old Mayfair property.

Askin's model home design is a credit to Habersham Way, a lovely tree-shaded byway of beautiful houses and gardens, mostly from the 1920s and '30s when traditionalism reigned supreme in Buckhead, much as it does today. Since Askins was, in a sense, his own client here, this house is a quintessential example of his work.

Current owners: Mr. and Mrs. James K. Christians

The garden façade on the facing page is a Mt. Vernon piazza with columns in the classic Temple of the Winds Order. The interior woodwork and plan reflects the Georgian style of late eighteenth-century England.

70

10 Habersham Way
Mayfair

In a curve of Habersham Way, almost hidden behind a graceful wall of white painted bricks, is this beautiful evocation of antebellum Georgia. Built in 1929 and originally called Mayfair, it has become one of Atlanta's most famous houses and was certainly one of the most elegant two-family dwellings in the city. Built to serve as the residence of the Henry Morrell Atkinsons and their daughter and son-in-law, the Jackson P. Dicks, Mayfair was carefully scaled to seem almost delicate and feminine rather than monumental. (Mayfair is an especially appropriate name, because both Mrs. Atkinson and her daughter were named May.)

The Atkinsons and the Dicks had separate private quarters. There were eleven bedrooms and eleven baths, yet the first floor could be thrown together to make one great house, focused on a curving staircase worthy of Scarlett O'Hara. Architecture was by the Atlanta firm Cooper & Cooper, landscape architecture by Ellen Shipman of New York, and interior decoration by Porter and Porter of Atlanta. Originally there were thirty-one acres, with formal gardens, a tennis court, and other luxury landscape features. Two well-landscaped acres still protect the estate's privacy.

Dr. and Mrs. Richardson have restored and furnished their historic Buckhead home to the past beauty its builders and architects envisioned in the late 1920s when it was first called Mayfair.

In 1954 Mayfair was sold to Mr. and Mrs. Alfred D. Kennedy, who made it a home for a single family and lived here until 1971, calling it Laurel Hill. Alfred Kennedy was president of the Atlanta Music Festival Association, which annually brought the Metropolitan Opera to Atlanta. Opera parties never had a more perfect setting, but the *ne plus ultra* of Mayfair evenings was the party the Kennedys gave here during the second premiere of *Gone with the Wind*. With film stars Vivian Leigh and Olivia de Haviland in attendance, Mayfair became Twelve Oaks, Tara, and Shangri-la all in one.

After the Kennedys, Mr. and Mrs. Steven H. Fuller Jr. renovated the house, which they also called Mayfair. Twice it was the Decorator's Show House of the Women's Association (Junior Committee) of the Atlanta Symphony Orchestra. When it belonged to Mr. and Mrs. Bert Lance, they entertained President and Mrs. Carter and other dignitaries from the Georgian's presidential administration.

The current owners, Dr. and Mrs. H. Dale Richardson, have restored Mayfair to a time when opera enlivened those elegant premises and the house was the setting for a movie premiere party at which for one evening the romantic legends of old Georgia seemed more real than fiction.

Current owners: Dr. and Mrs. H. Dale Richardson

With the Hardin's careful renovation, a Buckhead landmark home continues to be a classic Georgian revival presence at the Peachtree Heights crossroads of Habersham and West Wesley roads.

74

2730 Habersham Road

This is one of those rare Atlanta houses that has been home to only two families since it was built. To pass the corner of Habersham and West Wesley roads is to see a serene, unchanging redbrick and limestone Georgian revival presence, dark green mounds of boxwood, and a curving gray driveway gracefully ascending a little hill, which parts a perfect golf-green lawn. Mr. and Mrs. Otis Alvin Barge, who commissioned Ivey & Crook to design and oversee its construction in 1932, might still be at home.

This impression is exactly as the current owners, Mr. and Mrs. Allen S. (Bo and Sheri) Hardin Jr., would have it. Lewis "Buck" Crook houses can engender such loyalty. Perhaps that is why Ivey & Crook job number 276 still looks today, inside and out, faithfully as Buck Crook designed it and Ed Ivey supervised its building.

During the post-World War I decades in Atlanta, new suburbs were being formed in the affluent northwest and northeast sections, and a gracious house such as this reflects the trend toward suburban residential growth. Observers often praised these great leafy garden suburbs, with curving streets that follow and enhance the natural contours of the hilly terrain and broad avenues with landscaped medians and small wooded parks. The houses were built on fairly large, well-landscaped lots among neighboring residences of similar quality.

Ivey & Crook, with the best of their colleagues, provided a complete design service for a client who could afford to build in such suburbs. This service included a topographical survey to help in placing the house in the context of the vegetation, terrain, and neighborhood. The firm frequently presented the client with a landscape plan suggesting an overall scheme for the grounds and garden features.

Crook's 1932 design for the Barges imparted a timeless and serene majesty to 2730 Habersham that has not faded and has been respected to the present moment. The young Hardins appreciate what they have acquired and are making every effort to preserve and maintain it, at the same time that they enjoy their lives here, making it a warm and hospitable home for a growing family.

Current owners: Mr. and Mrs. Allen Sage Hardin Jr.

10 Cherokee Road

Dr. Cosby Swanson had this house built in 1922 at the corner of then-unpaved Vernon Road, on a large lot that he purchased for $4,000 in 1919 from the Peachtree Heights Park Company. It was just as the neighborhood began. At that time, the only other house on that side of Cherokee Road stood at number 28 near Habersham Road. The builder was the well-known Atlanta contracting firm of Herbert W. Nicholes (1871-1959) and his son Martin (1892-1982); later, H. W. Nicholes and Son would develop Collier Hills. The firm had a staff architect so that their house for Dr. Swanson was designed according to a professional plan.

When number 10 Cherokee was included on the Peachtree Heights tour of homes in the fall of 1994, it was called the Swanson-Van Meter House and given the suggestive designation "Italian revival." Certainly it is an early twentieth-century version of a villa, with its horizontality, low-pitched slate roof, bracketed eaves, and renaissance details, particularly the unit of the three arched windows separated by pilasters on the projecting front wing toward Vernon Road. A Swanson family scrapbook shows a formal rear garden, which no longer survives.

When the house was last purchased in 1983, the buyer wanted a house and neighborhood that would remind her of certain areas of Lexington, Kentucky, "a settled residential area with older homes." This was the fourth house her real estate agent showed.

In the 1960s the artist Comer Jennings, who lived nearby, suggested to a former owner that exterior shutters be added and the sunburst design over the front door be copied and placed in seven existing arches over the first-floor casement windows. At that time also, a frame addition, designed by architect Leon Lanier, enlarged the rear façade.

The owner is well satisfied with her choice of Atlanta neighborhoods, pleased to maintain the beauty of her home, one of the street's oldest, and its historic Peachtree Heights setting.

From the road, the house appears essentially as built in 1931. Inside are numerous changes and additions. This is the original staircase, but at right is a new family room added by the current owners.

330 Argonne Drive

The area where Argonne Drive forks off Habersham Road was part of the original Peachtree Heights Park, at least up to this house at number 330, built about 1931. As the street heads west toward Arden Road, the elevation begins to grow higher, and at 330 this house commands a low knoll. The first owner was Harold O. Rogers of the Rogers Grocery Company.

Almost immediately, in 1932, Walter H. Rich, president of Rich's Department Store during the decades before World War II, bought it. Rich, a civic leader of major proportions, a great man, really, moved here from Peachtree Circle in Ansley Park, and before that he lived in Druid Hills. Both his earlier homes had been designed by the legendary Neel Reid. (Mrs. Harry Norman Sr. was real estate agent for the Walter Rich estate in 1947.)

Great men, of course, are expected to live in great houses, like this one reminiscent of George Washington's Mt. Vernon. Washington had certainly set a notable example of that pattern of great houses for great men in the early days of the United States. Washington used a classical term, piazza, for his big southern sitting porch. Facing the Potomac River, Washington's piazza – he is considered its designer – created a tradition, especially during the colonial revival of the 1910s, '20s and '30s. It has been copied, in various degrees of authenticity, thousands of times. The columned piazza at Mt. Vernon inspired this one on Argonne Drive in Atlanta's Buckhead; it is a good example of the genre.

A house with this monumental entrance façade represents a southern architectural art form worthy of preservation and appreciation as a home in which to live the good life George Washington helped us secure. Others who have lived in this handsome house are Mr. and Mrs. Charles D. Collins and Mr. and Mrs. E. Reginald Hancock. The current owners are Mr. and Mrs. Larry Gerdes, who enlisted Buckhead architect Norman Askins for their recent renovations, which have made it a great house again.

Current owners: Mr. and Mrs. Larry Gerdes

3119 Habersham Road

The property along the east side of Habersham Road, from this house south to West Andrews Drive, began to be developed in the late 1920s. (Habersham from Argonne Drive is an extension from Peachtree Heights Park.) Number 3119, sited on the highest ground in the block, spreads along the ridge, a French Norman evocation on a two-acre estate of tall oak trees. Nearby, at the corner of West Andrews is another 1920s neighborhood manor, number 3053 Habersham. Both houses have asymetrical profiles, steeply pitched front-facing gables, and significant chimneys, evoking baronial, pre-eighteenth-century domestic architecture. They make an impressive pair of period houses, which reinforce the sense of this neighborhood as a historic suburb.

For many years this was the home of Mr. and Mrs. Cyrus E. Hornsby Jr., who bought the place in 1962. She was an interior decorator. Before that it was the home of Mrs. Mary O. Leatherman, who had it built. Mrs. Hornsby owned it until she died in 1996. The present owners cherish their all-too-short tenure and expect to raise their children here. They have lived in Atlanta off and on for eighteen years, but they are now committed to the history and convenience of Buckhead. During their extensive renovation, one of the treats of this house for them was finding in the basement old chandeliers, said to be from Atlanta's Biltmore Hotel, which they have had restored and installed.

The present owners of this Habersham Road medieval manor have lavished great efforts on renovating its inherent beauty, and expect to make it their home for many years as they raise their family here.

Architect Lewis Crook designed this Greek revival-style house in 1951 for the Fred Pattersons; it seems to bear out the architect's belief that "there are cycles in architecture, but people always return to the classics." The current owner, Charles Howard Candler III, finds it suitable for today's living.

82

2959 Andrews Drive

Lewis Edmund "Buck" Crook Jr. (1898-1967) of the Atlanta architectural firm of Ivey & Crook was a leading member of the Georgia school of twentieth-century classicists. This school was spawned when Neel Reid, Hal Hentz, and Rudolph Adler began practice in 1909-11 after they returned from architectural studies at Columbia University in New York and scholarly European travel. Both Lewis Crook and his partner, Ed Ivey, were protégés in the firm of Hentz, Reid & Adler after graduating in architecture from Georgia Tech and before they formed their own firm in 1923. Ivey & Crook job number 563, designed in 1951 for Fred W. Patterson, is 2959 Andrews Drive in the Peachtree Heights Park area of Buckhead.

In the past, leading Atlanta architects such as Ivey & Crook and Hentz, Reid & Adler practiced in the Candler Building built in 1906 on Peachtree Street. The current owner of 2959 Andrews Drive, Charles Howard Candler III, is the great-grandson and grandson of the owners and builders of the Candler Building, Asa Griggs Candler and Charles Howard Candler. The Candler family has contributed greatly to the Atlanta architectural scene, and that tradition continues in the present day.

Fred Patterson, the original owner of this house, who commissioned Ivey & Crook to design it, was also an important architectural client; he was the owner of H. M. Patterson and Sons Funeral Directors. Ivey & Crook also designed for him the Patterson's facility at Brookhaven known as Oglethorpe Hill (1957).

Lewis Crook devised a contemporary version of southern Greek revival architecture for Atlantans, red brick with white trim. This one for Fred Patterson is one of his finest.

Crook wrote that Greek revival was "our own great national style in architecture," expressing "a simplicity, a restraint, and an exquisite harmony that is needed in our modern architecture." No finer example of Crook's doing what he says can be found than Mr. Candler's home in Atlanta's Peachtree Heights. An original twentieth-century form of classical revival domestic architecture, 2959 Andrews Drive is being preserved and enjoyed today as Mr. Crook conceived it in the mid 1950s. As the late Buck Crook used to say, "There are cycles in architecture, but people always return to the classics."

Current owner: Charles Howard Candler III

15 Cherokee Road

Rawson Haverty reminisced about this place in his book *Ain't The Roses Sweet* (1989). It was his parents' home from 1927 until Mrs. Haverty's death in 1986. Rawson, born in 1920, grew up here from age seven, one of three children of Clarence (1881-1960) and Elizabeth Rawson (1889-1986) Haverty; he had two sisters, Clare and Elizabeth. The house had been built in 1923 as the home of Harold O. Rogers, who made a fortune in the grocery business. The plans were drawn by Robert S. Pringle, later of Pringle & Smith. After the death of Rogers, his family sold to J. Wick Goldsmith, who lived here for three years. Clarence Haverty swapped houses with Goldsmith.

There were several months of remodeling. A library was made from an open porch on the west elevation, and a little screened porch on the east was enclosed to make a sunroom. Rawson remembered that they all "loved 15 Cherokee." It was "home." They ate breakfast and lunch in a little breakfast room, but dinner was always served with the whole family in the dining room. He wrote, "It seemed perfectly natural to have a vegetable garden in the backyard and to keep chickens behind the garage." They had rabbits, grapevines, and fig trees. He recalled wonderful neighbors. He attended nearby E. Rivers school and then North Fulton High.

The Havertys owned the homeplace until his mother's death in 1986, when it was sold to Emmett Barnes Jr. Belle Turner Cross became the new owner in December 1989. A member of the Haverty family said to Mrs. Cross: "My mother would be so happy that someone dearly loves her house." There are 3.08 acres, and Belle Cross, an Atlanta native and expert gardener, knows every square foot of what has become her own homeplace, which she has put in perhaps the finest condition of its long life. She particularly wanted to restore the grounds, especially the rear gardens to the way they were when described as in the style of the Grove Park Inn at Asheville, North Carolina, with rock-bordered tile walks, small wooden bridges, rock walls and benches.

Cherokee Road is part of Peachtree Heights Park, known for a perfect combination of naturalistic landscape design and period revival domestic architecture. Cherokee Road has been called the prettiest street in Atlanta. No better example of the street's beauty could be found than this pink stucco, tile-roofed Mediterranean-style mansion, surrounded by its landscape-garden yard and golf course green lawn.

Current owner: Belle Turner Cross

3 Cherokee Road

This beautiful suburban house has become an Atlanta landmark. How does a house built fewer than a hundred years ago achieve such distinction?

In 1922 Jesse Howlett Draper and his wife, Constance Knowles Draper, had been married fewer than ten years when they had Neel Reid design for them this elegant early twentieth-century adaptation of a southern Greek revival cottage. Cherokee Road was only beginning to be developed as part of one of Atlanta's most desirable northside neighborhoods, and Jessie Draper (1885-1973) was beginning his long career as a popular Atlanta business, civic, and social leader. Among other achievements, he was a naval officer, founded the Draper-Owens Company, served as president of the Atlanta Historical Society, and was a city councilman from the Buckhead area. Constance Draper was one of Neel Reid's closest friends, a garden designer in her own right, and this house no doubt reflects her well-informed taste; she was a perfect Neel Reid client.

In 1978 when Cecil Phillips, an attorney, and his wife, Carol, acquired the house from the Drapers' estate, they had been in Atlanta a short time and were a young couple with a bright future, as the Drapers had been when the house was built. They decided that Neel Reid's and the Drapers' architectural conception was valuable and beautiful but that the second story must be made into more than an attic and the kitchen brought up to current standards. (The Drapers had had no children and lived only on the main floor.) The Phillipses and architect Ward Seymour over a period of years have made the Drapers' small and elegant house into a home for the way of life of a couple with children, a couple who have contributed to Atlanta from this home as the Drapers did in their era. Thus a fine Atlanta house became a landmark in fewer than one hundred years, even in fewer than eighty, and has the rare distinction of having had only two owners since it was built.

Current owners: Carol and Cecil Phillips

The unchanging beauty of this Habersham Road colonial revival-style landmark has been preserved outside, with interior changes that a new generation expects in a fine home today.

90

2628 Habersham Road

One of the wonderfully unchanging aspects of Habersham Road and its Buckhead neighborhood of Peachtree Heights Park is this landmark presence at the corner of Woodward Way. Built in 1926-27, it was the home of Mrs. William H. Schroder Sr. (Mary Elizabeth Barge) for nearly fifty years, until 1997. Mrs. Schroder had grown up in the neighborhood, at 2730 Habersham, the Otis Alvin Barge house, so it was natural that she chose this neighborhood in which to live and rear a family.

The Schroders purchased the house in 1951 when their son, Bill, was ten years old. They bought it from L. Neil Conrad. The house had been built for Mr. and Mrs. William B. Disbro Jr. Disbro, who sold it to Conrad in 1931, was in a family lumber business that specialized in fine millwork. That business explains why this is a well-built, handsomely finished house. The name of the original architect is unknown, but he was a talented designer in the colonial Georgian idiom.

One of the most distinctive features of its white-frame traditional style is the ground-floor pattern of fanlights over windows, repeated at the fanlighted recessed entrance, all tied together with arched black-green shutters and an arcaded porch, now glass enclosed, at the Woodward Way side of the façade. Mounds of deep green boxwood complete the green and white geometry of this satisfyingly unchanging composition.

Mary Elizabeth Barge Schroder had enjoyed much of her life in Peachtree Heights, having grown up in another one of the serene Georgian revival houses of the neighborhood. In 1997 she moved to a one-story house and sold her home to Lilla Costello, who made some interior alterations that reflect current needs, without changing the essential architecture that had attracted Mrs. Costello to this Habersham Road landmark in the first place.

Current owner: Lilla and M.E. Costello

2868 Andrews Drive

The original plans and specifications for this house show that it was designed for Alfred Doby Kennedy (1881-1950) by the Atlanta architectural firm of Pringle & Smith in 1924. Although the firm was new at that time, Francis Palmer Smith produced an accomplished, if straightforward, design in the collegiate Tudor-Gothic style. Francis Smith taught architectural design at Georgia Tech; he liked this revival style, which was used for buildings on the Georgia Tech campus in the 1920s.

At that time Alfred Kennedy was forty-three years old, a native of Camden, South Carolina, a Georgia Tech graduate, and a manufacturer of vegetable-oil machinery. His son, the late Alfred D. Kennedy Jr. (d. 1983), and grandson, Alfred D. Kennedy, have also been distinguished Atlanta citizens. (The home of Alfred D. Kennedy at 430 Argonne Drive is shown in this book on page 64.)

Characteristic of this old English style of redbrick architecture are steep roofs and gables, round and pointed arches, limestone trim, grouped windows, and asymmetrical facades. An architectural element that is an essential hallmark of the style is the porte cochere, meaning carriage porch. This house has one on the north elevation. Such a porch must be large enough for wheeled vehicles to pass through and to shelter passengers as they enter or exit vehicles.

Since 1993, Mr. and Mrs. Robert Parker have been the owners of this early Pringle & Smith example in Peachtree Heights Park.

Current owners: Mr. and Mrs. Robert A. Parker

Designed in 1924 in the Tudor-Gothic revival style, this house has handsome period details and materials throughout, such as the paneled and carved staircase.

109 West Wesley Road

On the Peachtree Heights Park subdivision plan by architect Carrere & Hastings of New York, 1910-11, revised in 1915 and 1925, West Wesley Road is just Wesley Drive and Vernon Road is Serpentine Drive. The property at the northwest corner of Wesley and Serpentine drives had been sold by 1925; in fact, almost all the plots throughout the development had been sold. That year was the height of the southern land boom and 1920s prosperity that began to close down only in the late 1920s.

Number 109 West Wesley was built in the midst of this boom by James Edwin Hickey, a native of Lynchburg, Virginia, who came to Atlanta in 1895 and died in 1929, leaving his widow here until she died in 1983. Hickey had been an investor and a board member of the old Trust Company of Georgia and the First National Bank of Atlanta. When Ada A. Hickey was "up in years," she built an enclosed swimming pool on the rear of her home to use for arthritis therapy.

The history of a house as it evolves into a home is the history of people, a changing cast and new scripts. The estate of Ada Hickey sold the place in 1983 to a pair of doctors, husband and wife M.D.s, the doctors Frank and Edna Copeland, who later sold it to the Kermit Birchfields.

The current owners' lifestyle suggests taking away Mrs. Ada Hickey's indoor exercise pool, definitely a somewhat unusual addition. But that is all they want to delete from the Hickeys' late 1920s redbrick Georgian revival-style period house, which is reminiscent of eighteenth-century Virginia manor houses in James Hickey's birthplace. The owners love its beautiful brickwork, the windows and dormers geometrically lined up around that elegant central pedimented doorway of carved limestone. They love its formal plan with the wide central hallway and the elegant Adam mantelpieces and other woodwork.

Anyone lucky enough to acquire one of these sorts of classic Georgian revival suburban mansions on which people lavished money and taste in the creation of a beautiful home wins an architectural lottery. They are a big responsibility, but worth it.

The living and dining rooms demonstrate the owners' genteel amalgamation of taste and elegance in the furnishing of this beautiful and architecturally significant house.

2690 Habersham Road

The garden suburb plan of Peachtree Heights Park assures the owners' privacy at 2690 Habersham. The façade elevation seen from Habersham Road is effectively the rear of the house, which faces Sibley Park and sits next to a portion of the park on its south elevation at the corner of Woodward Way. An old-fashioned glass conservatory, which the owners, Mr. and Mrs. Leonard Hultquist, placed on the Habersham Road side in 1995, houses a breakfast room that takes advantage of the views of Sibley Park to the east and to the south. The property originally had ten acres, but the two remaining seem like a national forest.

To underline and further that sense of seclusion, the main entrance to this Norman-French period revival mansion is hidden in the back garden and rear courtyard. One enters the house in the turreted tower, which is part of the original design by Albert Howell, architect, of Tucker & Howell. The entrance façade faces toward West Wesley Road and possibly may have originally been intended as a West Wesley address in the early days of Peachtree Heights. This was an early Tucker & Howell design when that firm was just starting out.

Designed in March 1934 for Julian Howell, the architect's younger brother, as the prosperity of the 1920s disappeared, it took a number of months to complete. Later it was the home of Robert M. Schwab and then of Spencer Boyd, a consulting engineer, until his death. The Hultquists bought it from Mr. Boyd's widow's estate and moved in during December 1995, after months of renovation, inside and outside, but always with respect for the original architectural character of the Tucker & Howell design. (They moved here from number 20 Cherokee Road. See pages 102-103.)

Mr. and Mrs. Hultquist like its French chateau charm and wooded setting. It seems far from the city – in the Normandy countryside – but is only blocks from Peachtree Road and the Buckhead shopping district. One of Buckhead's most romantic and picturesque homes, its private, naturalistic setting confirms the good suburban planning that went into the creation of Peachtree Heights some ninety years ago.

Current owners: Mr. and Mrs. Leonard Hultquist

The Leonard Hultquists have renovated and furnished their home in keeping with the French taste of the architect Albert Howell who designed it for his brother, Julian, in March 1934. (Mrs. Louise Huff, the late interior designer, helped them with the interiors.)

21 Cherokee Road

In 1923 Rybun Clay had Pringle & Smith, Architects, design this house for his family, as Peachtree Heights Park was being developed and close to the time Pringle & Smith went into practice, in 1922. It was quite a fine early project. Rybun Clay was president of the old Fulton National Bank (later Bank South and then NationsBank) for many years; he was a close business associate of Clarence Haverty, who lived next door at number 15. (Clay's daughter, Zaida, and Betty Haverty were the same age and best friends.) Rybun Clay's brother was the World War II era general Lucius Clay, who was a guest here many times.

Pringle & Smith was a versatile architectural firm led by partners Robert S. Pringle (1883-1937) and Francis Palmer Smith (1886-1971). Smith's architect son, Henry Howard Smith, who still operates the practice in 1999, says that this house was designed just after the practice began. Francis Smith was one of the founders of the architecture school of Georgia Tech. He was a very accomplished beaux arts designer who had studied with Paul Cret, the great teacher of architecture at the University of Pennsylvania, before Smith came to teach at Georgia Tech.

Pringle & Smith was a prolific firm; Francis Smith especially liked Gothic and other European precedents. This house, built in the American colonial revival style for the Clays, was somewhat of a departure for Smith. The front portico is inspired by George Washington's riverfront piazza for Mt. Vernon, one of the most influential of all American neoclassical prototypes. There are several other variations of this piazza form in Atlanta.

When this house was on the Atlanta Preservation Center's Peachtree Heights Tour of Homes in October 1994, there were six other homes along Cherokee Road on the tour; number 21 was called the Clay/Bostwick House.

Current owners: Jane and John Bostwick

Cherokee Road has been called "the prettiest street" in Buckhead, which is a fine accolade that this house, inside and outside, upholds every detail of its colonial revival style.

2590 Rivers Road

This late twentieth-century residence-pavilion found its inspiration in the late eighteenth-century French *pavillons* from the reigns of Louis XV and XVI. Since it was completed in 1988 for Mr. and Mrs. C. W. Close Jr., there have only been two other owners. Mary Close conceived it with the help of an Atlanta architectural designer, John Caldwell Calhoun, a traditionalist and classicist of the old school.

The flat, wedge-shaped lot of less than one-half acre, at the intersection of Rivers Road and Muscogee Avenue, is only a long block off Peachtree Road in the long-established Peachtree Heights neighborhood of Buckhead. It was a challenge and, some said, "unbuildable." The V-shaped corner lot helped determine the configuration of the pavilion, two one-story wings joined by a central entrance rotunda crowned by a low dome. Symmetry and craftsmanship reign in the classical tradition, as they do here.

John Calhoun has abstracted the essentials of period form and details. Note the touches of *treillage*, the French word for that old southern favorite, trellis-work. He found craftsmen who could execute what he indicated in his full-scale drawings done by hand in the old manner. The oval entrance hall, lighted from above with a domed skylight, opens into a light-filled living room lined with French doors leading to a small rear courtyard.

This residence is based on the sort of French neoclassical house that our southern architect president, Thomas Jefferson, took as his model for his own home, Monticello (little mountain), except that this is the reverse. It is a stylish pavilion house in a dell, amidst numerous other homes. The way it is sited and landscaped, however, gives it some of the privacy that Jefferson craved, for there are no immediate neighbors on either side.

The second owners were Dr. and Mrs. Ellis Jones, who moved from a large Philip Shutze house on Habersham Road, and the third and present are Dr. and Mrs. John C. Rieser. The Riesers came here from another eighteenth-century French-inspired house, a James Means design, that sits on a bluff above Peachtree Creek. They moved from their own secluded Monticello to this urbane pavilion in the vale of Rivers Road.

Current owners: Dr. and Mrs. John C. Rieser

French residence-pavilions of the mid-eighteenth century inspired this 1987-88 design by architect John Calhoun, which now has its third owner. Calhoun's elegant woodwork is complemented by the owner's equally elegant French furnishings.

Since this house was built in 1925 in the Mediterranean revival style, it has been steadily improved, without losing its period character. The refinements have only made it a more worthy contributor to the beauty and history of Peachtree Heights Park.

20 Cherokee Road

When the Atlanta Preservation Center and Harry Norman, Realtors, sponsored a Peachtree Heights West Tour of Homes in October 1994, this was one of nine houses open to the public on Cherokee Road and Andrews Drive in the residential heart of Buckhead. Seven of the houses on tour were designed by well-known Atlanta architectural firms, including two by the legendary Neel Reid of Hentz, Reid & Adler, one by Reid's protégé, Lewis Crook, of Ivey & Crook, one by the firm of Pringle & Smith, and this one at number 20 by Burge & Stevens. Clearly the neighborhood is architecturally affluent.

Dating from 1925, this house has been described as "Tuscan Italian," especially after it was renovated in 1992 by the architect Richard Dooley. The current owner, who purchased the house in 1995, had grown up nearby, so this was a "coming-home location," as a relative happily described it. (Two years of further renovations were completed before the owner occupied the house.)

James Dickey's famous 1969 poem "Looking for the Buckhead Boys" ("The Buckhead Boys. If I can find them, even one, I'm home,") memorializes a community that, in fact, has seldom actually used the term Peachtree Heights. The full original terminology was Peachtree Heights Park, which was later divided by Peachtree Road into West and East.

The E. Rivers Realty Company, headed by Eretus Rivers (1872-1932), had the New York firm of Carrere & Hastings, Architects, plan the subdivision in 1910-11. Rivers started his developer career in 1906 by purchasing several hundred acres of wild land astride Peachtree Road north of Peachtree Creek. The E. Rivers Elementary School at Peachtree Road and Peachtree Battle Avenue is named for him.

When number 20 Cherokee Road was built in 1925, the Rivers development was described as "one of the most popular suburbs of Atlanta, filled with fine homes representing an investment of many millions." In the year 2000, the area is still one of Atlanta's most popular, but that evaluation would now need to be changed to "billions." Today, there is little wild land left in this "coming-home location" in Buckhead that Mr. Rivers tamed into Peachtree Heights. Number 20 Cherokee Road well represents the beauty, stability, and success of his planning nearly a century ago. It is indeed a desirable location to come home to.

15 Austell Way

Austell Way was developed in the early 1920s during the extension of Peachtree Heights Park and Andrews Drive; it was named for pioneer Atlanta financier Gen. Alfred Austell. This sophisticated two-story brick house was built in 1924 on its two-acre plot, and it has been home to only four families. The architect was Owen James Southwell (1892-1962), a native of Louisiana who grew up in Beaumont, Texas; he came to Atlanta in 1914 with New York architect Harry Hornbostel, designer of the Emory University campus, and returned to Texas in 1931 after designing a number of important houses in Atlanta. (See 591 West Paces Ferry Road, page 134.)

Willis B. Jones, an interior decorator and the son of the outstanding physician-surgeon Dr. William B. Jones, purchased it in 1952. Jones's wife and widow, Nadine H. Jones, sold it in 1980 to Dr. and Mrs. Walter Ratchford. The Ratchfords built the present swimming pool, replacing a smaller pool from the Jones' era and have made many improvements, inside and outside.

Mrs. Ratchford notes she has in her possession the original plans of Hentz, Adler & Shutze and dated March 1, 1931, "for Miss Louise Fitton", for the addition of a garage and servants house, which has now been converted to a guest house. At that same time the firm converted the right end of the house from an open porch to a music room with a corner fireplace.

The dignified house clearly shows that Southwell was trained in the beaux arts tradition. The elegant entrance façade consists of a limestone frontispiece with a Palladian window and a broken pediment with a cartouche.

An interesting story Mrs. Ratchford passes on, but notes is "unconfirmed" is that the house was originally commissioned by an import tile dealer, whose business supplied tile for the Fox Theater. A tiled entrance room at the side of the house was reportedly designed and completed by some of the same designers and workmen from the Fox Theater crew. Such are the stories about a house that make it come alive, no matter how appealing the formal aesthetics of the architecture and landscape gardens may be.

Current owners: Dr. and Mrs. Walter Ratchford

555 Argonne Drive
Spotswood Hall

When this house was built in 1913, this acreage was in the country, and Buckhead did not extend this far away from the intersection of Peachtree, Roswell, and West Paces Ferry roads. Its builder, Shelby Smith, was chairman of the Fulton County Commission. His building site near Arden Road on a knoll within his sixteen-acre estate (now two acres) to this day commands a view of the Atlanta skyline to the south. His architect, a prominent Atlantan known for his civic buildings, was A. Ten Eyck Brown (1878-1940).

Most neoclassical domestic architecture ultimately derives from the works of the Italian Renaissance genius Andrea Palladio (1508-80). Spotswood Hall's classical pediment with columns derives from Palladio's trademark frontispieces for his private home designs, based on his understanding of ancient Roman architecture.

The house was given the name Spotswood Hall by its versatile second owner, Lucian Lamar Knight, a man of letters born in Atlanta in 1868. Knight was a writer for the *Atlanta Constitution*, an attorney, and an ordained Presbyterian minister. He wrote *Reminiscences of Famous Georgians* and became an associate editor of the *Atlanta Georgian*. When Knight purchased this place in 1917, he was leading a successful drive to establish an official state archives, and in 1918 he became the first director of the Georgia Department of Archives and History.

Dating from 1913 and a 1933 remodeling, Spotswood Hall is a well-preserved early Buckhead landmark, handsomely furnished with decorative arts appropriate to its early twentieth-century neoclassical architecture.

In 1930 Knight sold the estate for $50,000 to Walter C. Hill, a Retail Credit (Equifax) executive and a founder of the High Museum of Art. In 1932-33, Hill had Hentz, Adler & Shutze remodel and enlarge Spotswood Hall on the rear and inside. That the columned front elevation remains as designed by Ten Eyck Brown in 1913 is an enlightened early example of historic preservation. Philip Shutze replaced the stodgy original stairway with an elegant spiral and added a porte cochere on the north, with an entrance rotunda decorated with a chinoiserie mural painted by one of Atlanta's favorite artists, Athos Menaboni. It is still magically beautiful and is partially depicted on the overleaf of this book.

Spotswood Hall, a rare Atlanta residential landmark, truly has everything. Its current owners, Susan and Eric Friberg, recognize and appreciate it as a work of art and, in the spirit of preservation, maintain it as their own landmark home.

Current owners: Mr. and Mrs. Eric G. Friberg

3412 Knollwood Drive

Knollwood Drive connects Habersham Road and Peachtree Heights Park with Tuxedo Road and Tuxedo Park, north of West Paces Ferry Road. Some of the houses are less old than those in either of those surrounding neighborhoods.

Number 3412 Knollwood is a story-and-a-half horizontal house that started life in the 1960s as a slightly more formal version of what is usually called the ranch style: the all-American standby but with a French accent in some of the original details.

It was the underlying symmetry and formality that the youthful Atlanta traditionalists of the architectural firm of Spitzmiller & Norris have furthered and enhanced. It is a classicized version of its former self. The lone chimney has been enlarged, ornamentally reconfigured, and given a twin. But the most important added classical element is the well-proportioned pediment, with a half-moon fanlight in the tympanum, above the entrance. The horseshoe stairs have been retained, with a modified handrail. Matching dormers and four casement windows, all French in character, complement the other modifications, as do matching bays on the balancing wings. An open side porch with a Chinese Chippendale rail completes this façade lift, to coin a phrase.

The purpose of this expert cosmetic surgery, of course, is to give the house seasoned dignity, make it seem not less old, but more mature: a sophisticate and even an "antique." This subtle transformation was achieved for the owner, John Banks. Banks is a young man who wanted to complete the process at which the original builder only hinted: of realizing the Renaissance ideal of frontal order, bilateral symmetry, and visual delight. The operation was a success!

Current owner: John Banks

Refashioning a ranch-style house to complete the original builders intentions with more architectural flair has been achieved for John Banks. His furnishings complete the picture of elegance.

3656 Tuxedo Road

Charles H. Black Sr. organized the Tuxedo Park Company in 1911, later adding the Valley Road Company, to develop a large acreage along and north of West Paces Ferry Road. Blackland Road, within the area, is named for him. Eventually the development embraced five hundred acres. At first large country estates were the rule, but after 1920 Black began subdividing the land into somewhat smaller, yet still ample, building sites. He and his son, Charles H. Black Jr., both of whom lived in Tuxedo Park, built many of the houses here and along Valley and Blackland roads. Many of them were designed by the firm of Frazier & Bodin, Architects: D. H. Bodin (1895-1963) and C. E. Frazier (1886-1939).

In 1932 Charles H. Black Jr. built this residence for Mr. and Mrs. Charles B. Nunnally. It was one of a large number created by him, the team of Frazier & Bodin, and William Monroe Sr., of Monroe's Landscape and Nursery Company, who also helped plan and landscape the entire residential development.

Native Atlantan Charles B. Nunnally headed Nunnally and McCrea, a national distribution center for work clothes, together with his brother Hugh and T. H. McCrea. Catherine Smith Nunnally, his widow, lived here and at Sea Island until her death, when the house was placed on the market.

The Charles Nunnally house, with only minor changes inside and out, preserves the original 1932 conception. Atlanta classicist Clem Ford made some alterations in the mid-1960s. In 1996-97 the current owners, Mr. and Mrs. Hilton H. Howell Jr. had Norman Askins and his architectural associates, Yong Pak and James Jordan, make thoughtful modifications in the spirit of the original Frazier & Bodin design.

Robin and Hilton Howell respect the quality and history of the former Nunnally home and want only to enhance its beauty and livability. They have had expert suggestions from interior designer, T. Gordon Little. Robin Robinson Howell grew up in Tuxedo Park. She and Hilton, a Texan and adopted Atlantan, are enthusiastic about rearing their family at 3656 Tuxedo Road.

Current owners: Mr. and Mrs. Hilton H. Howell Jr.

The former Charles B. Nunnally home has been restored and renovated for the new owner, with expert professional help from notable architects and designers, comparable to the original talents that created it in 1932.

3800 Northside Drive

This long, horizontal country house is part of a 3.47-acre estate. The house began life in the late 1930s and then evolved from the original structure designed by Linton Hopkins Young (1910-98), for Mr. and Mrs. Ivan Allen Jr. Linton Young's scheme set the pace for later additions. The earliest part is the south end, where a fanlighted front doorway and rock-clad wall are located under a balconied verandah. Slender columnettes complete a charming picture of Young's "early American classicism" that has aged, and been added to, gracefully.

Lint Young was an Atlanta native, a fine Georgia Tech-trained architect. He was graduated with a B.S. in 1933 at age twenty-three, so this was an early work. He practiced for many years in the Candler Building among the preponderance of other Atlanta architects, including his elders, Lewis Crook and Philip Shutze, whose work Young admired and emulated.

Additions to the original scheme have been made by the Robert Chamberses (Anne Cox Chambers) in the 1950s and by Frank Carter in the 1960s. Both were owners for periods of time after the Ivan Allens built another house nearby, slightly south of here, on more of the land that Louise Richardson Allen's family had owned along Northside Drive for many years. Among the amenities of this picture-perfect setting, which has evolved since the 1930s, are formal gardens, a pool and pool house, and a lighted tennis court.

Current owners: Mr. and Mrs. Thomas Garic Moran

205 West Paces Ferry Road

One of the last great estate mansions built along Atlanta's suburban "Fifth Avenue," this house and its garden setting are maintained much as the architects Hentz, Adler & Shutze, and its original owners, the Albert Thorntons, conceived it in 1936. Dating from Atlanta's country-house era when Buckhead was still outside the Atlanta city limits, this house is smaller in acreage now (approximately 1.8), but the immediate grounds and gardens are still a perfect green Buckhead setting as designed. Today, at the same time, it is practically a townhouse as Buckhead has become less suburban and the nearby intersection of Peachtree, Roswell, and West Paces Ferry roads has become more popular than ever.

The architect Philip Shutze seemed to anticipate what happened to growing Atlanta in sixty years by designing this understated, formal rowhouse-like entrance façade visible to everyone. The more expansive American federal garden façade, featuring a charming columned portico, he placed privately in the rear away from the street.

To the left, as one enters the neo-classical front hall (semi-rotunda), is this paneled library recently given a faux finish.

With this house Philip Shutze gave late-eighteenth- and early-nineteenth-century English and American neoclassical architecture a fresh and charming interpretation: on the front, the Regency manner of the English architect Sir John Soane (1753-1837) and on the rear, the stucco neoclassicism of Augusta and Savannah, much of which was ultimately derived from Soane's influence.

Shutze set a stylish high standard here for the domestic architecture of Atlanta. A Georgia native, he was an exact contemporary of Edna Thornton, who was an Atlanta native with deep Wilkes County, Georgia, roots. When the Georgia Fine Arts Committee was formed in the mid-1960s to create the governor's mansion, Edna Thornton was chosen chairman of furnishings. In 1968, she expressed her standards for the project in the words, "It's a question of quality and taste, not money!" This was the standard she and her husband used in working with Hentz, Adler & Shutze to make their own home.

A series of such Atlantans has appreciated this visible West Paces Ferry landmark and preserved its integrity as they have made it their own home.

Current owners: Mr. and Mrs. William R. Dawson III

281 Blackland Road
Peninsula House

The Atlanta architectural firm of Frazier & Bodin built this lovely house at 281 Blackland Road in 1936 for Hugh Pendleton Nunnally, who had purchased the property from Charles Black, Sr. developer of Tuxedo Park. Bodin was a strong force in persuading the Nunnallys to position the house 500 feet from the street and to carve out a vista from the road to the house.

Atlantans have always loved this Georgian colonial style residence built of white brick with a pedimented entrance, Corinthian columns, and a leaded-glass fanlight above the doorway.

A circular staircase was the focal point of the entrance hall where handblocked Zuber wall covering was installed with such infinite attention to detail that when Mrs. Nunnally discovered that the seams did not match precisely, she hired an artist to paint over them to coordinate the design.

The house was the scene of parties in the gardens, sled rides and games, formal dinner parties, and many social galas. In 1939, when Clark Gable and his wife Carole Lombard were in Atlanta for the premiere of *Gone with the Wind*, promotional photographs of the Gables were taken with the home as the background. The house also starred in a 1948 article in *Life* magazine and appeared on the cover of a United Airlines timetable.

Mr. Nunnally died in 1953, and twenty years later his widow married Charles H. Black Jr. In 1977, Mary Lee Nunnally Black sold the house to His Royal Highness Prince Faisal M. Saud Al Kabir of Saudia Arabia who had come to Fort Benning for a military training program. It was Prince Faisal who gave the home the name it still carries, Peninsula House.

The prince asked Columbus architect Edward W. Neal to remodel the residence and Atlanta interior designer Ed Kilby furnished it with English and French pieces from the 18th century.

The prince and his wife, Princess Aisya, were lovely additions to the Atlanta social scene, and many fortunate guests were delighted with invitations to the beautiful residence. The prince eventually returned to Saudi Arabia, and a series of residents have since cherished the home. The current owners are in the process of adding their own sense of style and elegance to this landmark home. *Copy courtesy of Harry Norman, Realtors.*

As it is today, this estate with its classical house and extraordinary gardens, represents the sort of place envisioned for Tuxedo Park when the suburb was planned over seventy-five years ago.

3639 Tuxedo Road

The prospectus for the Tuxedo Park Company in 1931 shows how the neighborhood was laid out just north of the estate of Robert F. Maddox, which fronted on West Paces Ferry Road and extended toward Tuxedo Road. Tuxedo Park was largely carved out of Maddox's land by Charles H. Black, whose prospectus described the area as a preserve for fine residential architecture and natural beauty. Although Black's writer outdid himself, there is some truth in what he wrote: "Nature has been lavish with her gifts to Tuxedo Park. There are purling rills and murmuring streams that follow the winding course through budding trees, wild shrubs, and flowers, away from the noise, dirt and heat of the city. This beautiful property with its rolling hills of virgin forest has every alluring natural attraction."

Number 3639 Tuxedo Road could be presented today as the fulfillment of that prospectus from nearly seventy years ago. Built by Mr. and Mrs. Alton M. Costley in the early 1940s, their ownership ended in 1990. At that time, it became the home of the Rex Fuquas, followed by a lengthy renovation directed by Norman Askins's firm. Askins says that he added two large wings for Fuqua. The present owners had Askins double the square footage and subsequently he has made a new addition for them on the east elevation that includes a giant classical order that cannot be seen from the street.

Many new features of the house that seem appropriate to the neighborhood and to the house are Askins's designs, especially the Ionic entrance porch, purposefully overscaled – as Neel Reid often did – to create just the right flair of domestic monumentality appropriate for this "black-tie" park.

The natural beauty of the area is expressed in the rear gardens, a naturalistic landscape that has been included many times on tours and in books and magazines. These were developed by John Williams's Post Properties landscape gardeners. It is as though those who have created this setting had read Charles Black's dreams for his neighborhood.

1145 West Paces Ferry Road
White Oaks

Holiday magazine featured Atlanta in January 1951 with the North Carolinian James Street's famous line about Atlanta: "shrewd, proud and full of gumption, her Confederate slip showing under a Yankee mink coat." Atlanta, he said, was "a showcase of homes, commerce and cash." Within Street's article is a full-page photograph of the front of 1145 West Paces Ferry, guests arriving for a party.

Built in 1935, this was the home of Mr. and Mrs. Bolling Jones Jr. for most of its history. It is one of only a few mansions built in Buckhead in the Greek revival style. There were none here in the antebellum period, because this part of Atlanta was only sparsely settled until "after the War" and then by small farmers in plantation-plain frame houses. After Bolling Jones, president of the Atlanta Stove Works, died, his widow, Dorothy Hodgson Jones, lived here for many years. (Her sister was Nell Hodgson [Mrs. Robert] Woodruff.) After her death it went to the Second Ponce de Leon Baptist Church, which sold it to the current owners.

The new owners allowed it to be used as the 1998 Decorators' Show House of the Atlanta Symphony Orchestra. At that time, the house was described in this way: "Graced by a soaring portico with immense Doric columns that overlook a sweeping lawn, it has an elegant formal garden and a glass conservatory; the exterior is surrounded by oak, beech, magnolias and dogwood trees and numerous native shrubs."

Like its fellow West Paces Ferry Road house at number 205, this is a great Buckhead estate (3.5 acres) that has not greatly changed in appearance since the mid-1930s. As James Street suggested, 1145 West Paces Ferry has been one of the traditional bastions of social Atlanta. Today it could still be photographed to represent Atlanta as a place of southern beauty and pride, although we can be certain that if Dorothy Hodgson Jones ever wore a Yankee mink coat, her slip would have been properly in place, Confederate or not.

3430 Tuxedo Road

Tuxedo Road is a long suburban street that begins at West Paces Ferry Road, turning and bending until it crosses Blackland Road. It then proceeds more directly to its ending at Powers Ferry Road, near Chastain Park. According to an Atlanta Historical Society book about life in Atlanta from the 1940s to the 1970s, the Tuxedo Park area continued to be the location of some of the city's highest-priced residential real estate, a "bastion of wealth and prestige."

Number 3430 Tuxedo Road is near West Paces Ferry in the historically most prestigious part of Tuxedo Park, where the great period revival mansions for the 1920s and early 1930s were built for noted business and community leaders, after designs by noted architects. Building sites were large, and most of the wooded sites were easily adapted to the preferred traditional domestic architectural types set at the end of deep landscaped yards.

An exception once on this site was a modernistic, poured-concrete house, which the northside builder Vernon Marchman constructed as his own family home in the 1950s. Marchman dared to experiment with a flat roof and many of the other hallmarks of modernism. Almost hidden in the trees, the structure was a "concrete tree house." By the postmodern late 1970s such post-World War II modernism, even as an experiment, was not appealing in Tuxedo Park. Real estate entrepreneur Marcia Lyle purchased the place and in fourteen months had completely transformed it with the help of Todd Corbet. This young architect, like Ms. Lyle and many of their compatriots at that time, admired the work of Sir Edwin Lutyens, the brilliant early twentieth-century English architect whose inventive country houses were original statements of romantic traditionalism, harmoniously integrated with the landscape.

A comfortable, Lutyens-like synthesis of formality and picturesque naturalism was Marcia Lyle's ideal. Her dramatic transformation of 1950s modernism into 1970s postmodernism instantly appealed to Daniel and Patricia McGlaughlin, who still make it their home after nearly twenty years. They have a romantic château in the midst of Tuxedo Park's tall, well-tended shade trees.

Current owners: Pat and Dan McGlaughlin

65 Valley Road

Only three families have made this picturesque twentieth-century medieval manor their home since Samuel Candler Dobbs Jr. had it built in 1930. A distinguished Atlanta architectural firm, Cooper & Cooper, designed it for Mr. Dobbs, who called it Markan Hall.

Samuel Inman Cooper, FAIA (1894-1974), was an Atlanta native and a fellow of the American Institute of Architects. Cooper once remarked quite sensibly: "A building is a merging of art and function; it is more than a visual impression on the beholder. It is erected primarily for a purpose, often a useful purpose."

Samuel Candler Dobbs Jr. had in mind building a residence that would be both beautiful and functionally useful, one that would make a favorable impression on beholders, purposes it continues to achieve seventy years later.

The second residents were Mr. and Mrs. Albert I. Love, from the early 1940s into the 1970s. Mr. Love owned Foote and Davies, the Atlanta printing company.

After a very bad fire that destroyed the southwest wing and damaged other sections with smoke and water, the Edward Elsons, the third owners, came to the rescue and brought their architect friend Irv Weiner in to help them. The library's linen-fold paneling and Elizabethan plasterwork ceiling survived the fire more or less unscathed, but some of the Tudor-Gothic revival work had to be reconstituted. Even so, the place, which the Elsons named Rhododendron Hall, still resembles Sam Cooper's inspiration, Hever Castle, the ancestral home of Anne Boleyn.

Constructed of bricks, half-timbering, and warm stone, 65 Valley Road is another credit to Tuxedo Park, Charles Black's Buckhead development from the 1920s and 1930s. The present owners, Christie and Bob Cohen, have made this great baronial hall (on its 9.5-acre estate) their own home and castle in which to raise their family. Mrs. Cohen says that they only "want to bring out the original beauty of the house and grounds." In that regard, they have had the interior painted surfaces cleaned of all old coats of paint to reveal details before repainting, and the exterior has been carefully steam-cleaned to freshen the beautiful old stonework.

Current owners: Christie and Bob Cohen

This magnificent Tudor revival mansion built in 1930 on the scale of a baronial estate is now restored, landscaped, and furnished by its fourth owner in a manner both worthy and noble.

3640 Tuxedo Road

This house, the residence of Mr. and Mrs. Charles H. King, was featured in a prospectus that Charles H. Black published for the Tuxedo Park and Valley Road companies in the mid-1930s. Frazier & Bodin were the architects, C. H. Black Jr. was the builder, and the landscaper was Monroe's Landscape and Nursery Company. The exterior design of the lengthy two-story home is surprisingly restrained, Regency, with low-profile pilasters and white-painted bricks.

The Kings lived here from 1937 until it became the home of Mr. and Mrs. Robert Winship Woodruff in 1947. They moved here from Druid Hills, where they had lived in a Neel Reid house at 1196 Springdale Road. Their near neighbor, Catherine Nunnally, once graciously jested, "I am not Bob and Nell Woodruff's neighbor, they are mine; I was here first!" The Nunnallys had moved to Tuxedo Road in 1932, the Woodruffs in 1947.

In 1948, the Woodruffs' new residence was featured on the annual spring house and garden tour benefiting Egleston Hospital. It was also included on this charity tour in 1949 and again in 1953. At that time First Lady Mamie Eisenhower sent the Woodruffs a centerpiece decoration of "lace coral and sea fans" for their dining room table. In 1958 the living room and the grand marble-floored foyer were featured in Helen Comstock's book *100 Most Beautiful Rooms in America*.

When Robert Woodruff moved here he was fifty-nine years old and in his prime as head of the Coca-Cola Company, which his family and others had purchased from the Candlers and reorganized just after World War I. This house was his home until he died at age ninety-five in 1985.

Following the Charles Kings, the Robert Woodruffs, and the Robert Watts, the current owners have come to love 3640 Tuxedo Road as their home. They are keeping this house well placed on the map of Atlanta, adding to the growing honors of an already distinguished history.

591 West Paces Ferry Road
Dellbrook

An article in the *Atlanta Journal-Constitution* on September 29, 1988, described Tuxedo Park as "the Camelot of Atlanta's residential areas, with picture book mansions, rolling green acreage, and wooded backdrops." In the spring of 1999, the *Wall Street Journal* characterized Dellbrook, at Northside Drive and West Paces Ferry Road, as one of those Atlanta picture-book mansions.

Dellbrook is one of the last houses designed by Owen James Southwell (1892-1962) in Atlanta. Southwell came to Atlanta in 1914 with New York architect Henry Hornbostel, designer of the Emory University campus plan and its first marble-faced buildings in Druid Hills. He left in 1931, after having designed several large houses, including this one for Mr. and Mrs. Marcus M. Emmert, built in 1928-29. The interiors of the Emmerts' house were decorated by one of Atlanta's classic design firms, Porter & Porter; a detail of the stairhall shows scenic wallpaper similar to that in place in the house today.

An advertisement for the house in *Town & Country* magazine placed by Mrs. Harry Norman Sr. & Associates shows the entrance façade and automobile forecourt facing West Paces Ferry Road. The ad reads: "Tuxedo Park Estate. Located on over five acres [now 4.2] of gardens and forest. . . . The Georgian residence has a wide front-to-rear entrance hall with circular staircase. Spacious formal living room, paneled library, banquet dining room and family dining room, butlers pantry and sun room. There are five bedrooms and five and a half baths. . . . Exquisite detail prevails throughout."

A visit to the Lowe's house is like a step back in time when Buckhead mansions were being designed, landscaped, and furnished by the South's finest talent. People were celebrating the prosperity of the New South, while looking to the style of the Old.

The garden façade, which faces north, is shown in Charles Black's 1931 prospectus for his new Tuxedo Park development. An open loggia with Mt. Vernon-like square pillars overlooks a terraced garden and reflecting pool shaded by cherry trees, all of which are in place today. The character of the architecture is American Georgian revival.

The current owners, Mr. and Mrs. Thomas M. Lowe, have furnished their home in spirit much as it was when the Marcus Emmerts built it and Porter & Porter decorated it with antiques and fine paintings appropriate to a period house of the 1920s in Atlanta.

The Lowes purchased Dellbrook in 1975 when the larger Buckhead mansions were not in as much demand as they are today. Mr. Lowe, a Fulton County Commissioner, has seen Atlanta, the county seat, become the focus of new development and growth as people begin to desire living inside the Perimeter highway, again, in great style such as we see in his own home.

Current owners: Mr. and Mrs. Tom Lowe

138

1040 West Conway Drive

This three-story Regency-inspired home was built as the 1998 Holiday showhouse, a charitable project of retailer Neiman Marcus and *Southern Accents* magazine. Mr. and Mrs. John Smart purchased the home and took occupancy in March 1999. The Smarts moved to Atlanta several years ago. Their first Atlanta home was the well-known Philip Shutze-designed Kiser house, Knollwood, at West Paces Ferry and Woodhaven roads across from the governor's mansion.

The original design team for the twelve-thousand-square-foot residence was made up of Harrison Design Associates, architecture; John Oetgen, interiors; and Hugh and Mary Palmer Dargan, landscape architecture. The builders were Deane Johnson and Richard Williams.

Sited on the edge of a former pasture in a neighborhood called Mount Paran/Northside, this is the sort of traditional period revival-style house Atlantans admire. Popular in Georgia in the early nineteenth century, especially at Savannah in the work of the English-born architect William Jay, the classic Regency style has been brought into the twenty-first century here, quite effectively and convincingly. Regency has been considered a proto-modern style, classical but functional and almost streamlined, inventive, and surprising, with curved and mirrored walls and large windows that bring the outside in.

This neighborhood north of Nancy Creek, west of Northside Drive, and south of Mount Paran Road has been called a botanical Eden. Almost across from here are two lakes remaining from the old Dr. Charles Yarn property, the former home of the late Jane Hurt Yarn, who helped give the neighborhood its longtime reputation as a nature preserve. The Smarts' place, partially screened from the road and backing up to a green meadow with a forest beyond, little disturbs the quiet, naturalistic calm long enjoyed in the neighborhood. The warm beige color of the bricks seems at home in this setting.

Current owners: John and Pam Smart

This residence designed by the distinguished Atlanta architectural firm Jova Daniels Busby is a work of residential art that synthesizes classicism and modernism, the old and the new, into an original background for contemporary life.

30 Finch Forest Trail

The designer of this house, Stanley Daniels, was a founding partner of Jova Daniels Busby in 1966. One partner, John Busby, has been national president of AIA; the other, Henri Jova, was a Rome Prize fellow at the American Academy in Rome, Italy. Jova Daniels Busby is a large diversified practice. One of its early projects was Colony Square on Peachtree and Fourteenth streets in Midtown Atlanta. The firm has an interior design division, an early specialty in line with its goal of providing comprehensive design services.

Jova Daniels Busby would agree with the great New York architect Philip Johnson that one cannot not know and use history in designing buildings. That is why this house from 1982-83 in northwest Atlanta – sited among two acres of old trees – brings to mind various historical precedents, abstracted into an exciting and original expression. Their work mixes classicism and modernism (note the glass bricks), the old and the new.

The current owners' well developed sense of style meshes dramatically with their important contemporary art collection. Designer, Pamola Powell, presents an interior design scheme which uses bold colors, textures and finishes to integrate the collection. Certainly, this Atlanta residence is a showpiece.

4270 Harris Trail

This residence, which was designed in 1983 as the home of Charlotte and Rankin Smith Sr., was not considered absolutely complete until 1988 when it was unveiled in the house & garden section of the *Atlanta Journal-Constitution*. The writer of the article said that Charlotte Smith wanted a house that "looked like it had been there for years," and Rankin, the Falcons' owner, wanted the ample spread of ten acres of land in northwest Atlanta away from a more congested Buckhead, where they were living.

The Smiths purchased the land in 1976 and hired Frank McCall of Moultrie, Georgia, to be their architect. The newspaper account described McCall as "the heir to the illustrious design legacy of Neel Reid and Philip Shutze."

McCall said in 1988, "They wanted a classical house, authentic in detail, but they didn't want columns." He showed them photographs of English Regency, which they liked. A grand staircase was essential, as were high ceilings, both of which they got. From the combined vision of the Smiths and Frank McCall's firm (the project architect was John S. Hand), a 13,000-square-foot twentieth-century Regency house was fashioned. Mrs. Smith used furnishings she had collected for years and special pieces she selected with the help of her interior decorator of many years, Betty Sherrill, president of McMillan, Inc., in New York.

The house had been prominently featured on the dust jacket and in the text of William R. Mitchell Jr.'s 1992 book on the architecture of Frank McCall. Earlier, a May 1990 *Architectural Digest* article had presented the house and its garden setting to a large national audience. There Charlotte Smith described her home as "airy in the daytime, cheerful at night, never seeming to be crowded, and looking as if it had been there for years." Her vision was indeed realized.

Current owner: Mrs. Charlotte Topping Smith

This classical cabana was designed by Norman Askins after the house was built.

145

11706 Mountain Park Road

Roswell is an unusually appropriate place for building a new house that thoughtfully imitates the Greek revival of antebellum Georgia. Roswell King, for whom the town is named, led a group of coastal Georgia families here in the late 1830s to colonize former Indian lands just north of the Chattahoochee River. These colonists all built temple-form classical revival homes, which today constitute the town's historic district. Many years ago, national historians discovered this group of beautiful white-columned houses from the 1840s in Roswell, because Pres. Theodore "Teddy" Roosevelt's mother, Martha "Mittie" Bulloch, grew up at Bulloch Hall and was married there a few years before Southerners like the Bullochs, and Yankees like the Roosevelts, went to war. As an act of family piety and sectional reconciliation, Pres. Teddy Roosevelt made a famous visit to Bulloch Hall in 1905, focusing national attention on Roswell's white columns.

Mr. and Mrs. Cliff Conrad are responsible for this re-creation designed and built for them by the late John Baxter; it was his last house project. To build a house that could stand up to the antebellum originals in the Roswell Historic District required the sort of taste, information, and experience – and clients – that house-builder, designer, and antiquarian John Baxter had. He approached his projects like the late James Means, from the ground up, from seasoned materials to boxwood gardens, antique hardware and light fixtures. He based the plan on that of Bulloch Hall: a wide central hallway off which large rooms open.

The Conrads and Baxter merged history and the present: heart pine beams and hardwood floors, pocket doors, and a library with lots of shelves are balanced with a swimming pool, cabana and spa, and bathrooms and a kitchen that are certainly improvements on those that were found in the backyard in Mittie Bulloch's day.

Current owner: Toni Conrad

632 Mimosa Boulevard
Holly Hill

The Roswell town square is like a New England village green. Facing the square is this graceful Greek revival-style cottage of white-painted Georgia pine. Called a raised cottage and built about 1845, it has matching front and rear porticoes, with fluted columns in the Doric order. Located on the old main residential street, it stands on some three acres that slope gently west, affording wooded views from the high rear porch – a prospect seemingly far removed from the bustle of life in present-day Roswell.

Originally Holly Hill was the summer home of a Savannah cotton broker, Robert Adams Lewis, and his wife, Catherine Barrington Cook. Roswell King, the town's founder, was Mrs. Lewis's uncle, and Holly Hill was among the first houses that King and his son, Barrington, constructed during the 1840s in the vicinity of the square. Among other nearby survivors from that early date are Barrington, Mimosa, and Bulloch halls and Primrose Cottage.

The main, or parlor, floor is reached by ascending to the front portico on broad steps centered on a double door, with transom above. This handsome architectural feature leads into a wide central hall extending to the rear porch. The hall passes what were double parlors, two bedrooms, and a curved staircase. (The basement level held the original kitchen, dining room and pantry.) Classical ornamentation from the 1840s is intact; among the best of this is a pair of imported parlor mantels of black marble.

Although Robert and Catherine Lewis continued to use the house until travel became difficult during the War Between the States, in 1854 they had sold it to Barrington King's son, James. Thereafter a series of owners kept Holly Hill essentially as it had been originally. Important in its preservation were Robert L. and Evelyn Hanna Sommerville (now both deceased), who carefully renovated it as their home in the early 1950s.

The Sommervilles bought Holly Hill at the suggestion of an early historic preservation leader, the late Granger Hansell of neighboring Mimosa Hall. The three were part of a long line of people who have bequeathed Roswell's antebellum heritage to the present, and Holly Hill is one of the authentic landmarks of that heritage.

Current owners: Mr. and Mrs. Lewis Gray

Holly Hill is one of the original houses built in Roswell in what is now a historic district listed in the National Register of Historic Places.

This large villa overlooking the Chattahoochee River was conceived in the grand tradition of Atlanta estates from the 1910s and '20s. The staircase duplicates a Neel Reid design from 1915.

60 Sherington Place

Dunwoody is in the northeastern suburbs of Atlanta, mostly in DeKalb County, just north of the Perimeter Highway. The Chattahoochee River borders the northern edge of the neighborhood, and Sandy Springs, an unincorporated community in northern Fulton County, is just to the west of Dunwoody Village.

One of the most important and expensive houses ever built in this area graces a thirteen-and-one-half-acre wooded bluff on the south bank of the Chattahoochee River in Fulton County. It was finished in 1989 for Mr. and Mrs. Harry J. Butler Jr. Their advisor was David W. Meroney Jr., an Atlanta-based designer who directed the project. Subsequent owners have made extensive alterations, but it was the Butlers who actually created the house and the street out of a larger acreage. They had Meroney model their dream home on the old Bolling Jones house at 1145 West Paces Ferry Road (see page 124), largely because of the Jones' massive Greek Doric portico, an exterior feature here that remains unchanged. The grand interior double staircase also remains, a near duplication of Neel Reid's design for the old James Dickey house also on West Paces Ferry.

The current owner renovated the house as his Atlanta residence. His work enriched a place already quite deluxe into a belle epoque European country house hardly to be equaled in the region. There is even a large, temperature-controlled wine cellar.

The naturalistic landscape of this extensive Chattahoochee River preserve is entirely fenced; there are a guesthouse, a heated swimming pool with cabana and a nature trail along the riverbank. Despite the beauty of the staircase in the marble-floored reception foyer, an elevator reaches all levels of this European-American's grand twelve-thousand-square-foot villa.

1710 Marlborough Drive

The name Dunwoody came into this part of metropolitan Atlanta before the name Atlanta itself. The first of the local Dunwoodys spelled it Dunwody, as do his descendants. John Dunwody (1786-1858) and his wife, Jane Bulloch, came with the first settlers of Roswell in the late 1830s. John Dunwody and Jane built Mimosa Hall, and Jane's family built Bulloch Hall in what is now the Roswell Historic District.

Much of the Dunwoody community is in northwest DeKalb County. Always described as a great place to raise a family, Dunwoody is an upscale, affluent suburb, perhaps typified by this house at 1710 Marlborough Drive, which is set on over an acre of land overlooking the ninth fairway of the Dunwoody Country Club.

The design and execution resulted from a fine team made up of the late noted house designer John Baxter, builder Paul Gann, and the original owners, Mr. and Mrs. Gerard O. Carbonara, making suggestions. Completed in 1983 for the Carbonaras, who still live nearby, the home was inspired by late colonial New England precedents, which John Baxter excelled in duplicating, in form and in minute detail throughout. Among the special features are century-old heart-of-pine floors from an antebellum warehouse in downtown Atlanta. The landscape architects were Daugherty/Anderson and Associates; Rick Anderson was the project designer. The Carbonaras raised four children here, around its back garden swimming pool. Before they sold it to the Fowler-Kennedy household in 1993, they had modified the plan somewhat to open up the living spaces for an expanding family life.

Today, the entire scheme for this beautiful Dunwoody home has aged gracefully. The cedar shake roof, gray-blue shingles, and stonework have the patina of the antique New England prototypes that were its inspiration; it has all grown more beautiful here from the years of seasoning since 1983. John Fowler and his wife, Dr. Eimar Kennedy, have raised three children here and entertained a neighborhood of their friends around the family "swimming hole." Fowler says it is a wonderful suburban home, which company often thinks has been there far longer than the actual sixteen years because of the patina of its charming early-American style.

Current owners: Mr. John Fowler and Dr. Eimear Kennedy

Traditional architecture and interiors have been a Dunwoody hallmark. House designer John Baxter was expert at recreating the spirit of older homes, without sacrificing modern comfort and amenities.

8285 Jett Ferry Road

Jett Ferry Road is named for one of the earliest pioneer families of that part of north Fulton County near the Chattahoochee River. The Jetts came into the area in 1820, when what is now called Dunwoody was part of a larger Gwinnett County. The Gwinnett County census of 1820 lists James and Stephen Jett, the pioneer progenitors of this family. Jett Ferry, like a number of old roads in the Atlanta area, bears the name ferry because of the river crossings: Paces Ferry, Defoors Ferry and Montgomery Ferry, among others.

Number 8285 Jett Ferry Road was completed in 1993. There are twenty-three rooms on three main levels with approximately fifteen thousand square feet of living space. There is an elevator to all floors, an attached three-car garage, a swimming pool, and a tennis court. Design is a post-modern simplification of pre-Renaissance English and French domestic architecture.

One of the highlights of this home is the owner's "Grammy Room", displaying his collection of awards.

A place such as this seems in the mold of the spectacular mansions from the Gilded Age, hallmarks of the great nineteenth-century business entrepreneurs, not exact in style, of course, but in its luxurious amenities, materials, and spaciousness. More than a home, it is a work of domestic architectural art: there is nothing humble about these expansive custom-designed premises fit for a contemporary entrepreneur such as the present owner. Just as with the turn-of-the-century stately homes, there is a billiard room paneled with cherry and complemented by fabric panels along the upper walls. A state-of-the-art media room with a home theater and a multi-room sound control and security center for the entire estate fill a modern executive's needs.

Wouldn't the pioneer Jett family be surprised to see what has transpired on their old "stomping grounds"? From the Jetts, with their ferry across the Chattahoochee, to the Dunwoody international jet and tennis set, in little more than a century!

The current owner has made this a gated estate totally enclosed and elaborately landscaped with new interior décor.

4028 River Ridge Chase

River Ridge Chase is a cul-de-sac off Paper Mill Road in Cobb County that comes to an end at this secluded house nestled on a ledge above Sope Creek, a tributary of the Chattahoochee River. The name was once spelled Soap, which is believed to refer to soapstone. Near here is a four-hundred-acre National Recreation Area with woodlands and the stabilized ruins of the old Marietta Paper Mill (1859).

The Coopers' two picturesque acres slope to the creek and continue over to the far bank. Mrs. Cooper says it is like living in the north Georgia mountains. The five thousand square foot house designed to relate to the rocky creek below took twenty-two months and "183,000 bricks" to complete.

The Coopers chose their architects, Surber, Barber & Mooney, because they liked plans that firm was making for a Neel Reid-designed carriage house at the Winship Nunnallys' estate on West Paces Ferry Road. The project architect for their home was Kemp Mooney.

The site helped determine the design. It has, for example, nine sets of double doors opening to the setting. Mooney said he had in mind the work of a great early twentieth-century English architect, the eccentric Sir Edwin Lutyens (d. 1944), who often made the best of a picturesque site such as their ledge above Sope Creek. His houses, like this one, were carefully detailed and often set into and surrounded by a landscape garden. The builder was Sheldon Simms; the landscape designer was Allen Struletz.

Tom Cooper is a specialist in bariatric medicine (baros, or weight). Sharon Cooper is a state representative from Cobb County. This is a very personal house, truly a home created for and by the Coopers. Whimsical bears of the plump and friendly Pooh variety are at home in the Coopers' lair: there is a "Pooh Playhouse Tower" housing the swimming pool machinery below and a sculptured set of dancing bears down by the falling water of Sope Creek shoals.

Current owners: Dr. and Mrs. Tom Cooper

A bear by the front door introduces a favorite theme of Dr. and Mrs. Cooper for the home they have created above Sope Creek; he is a specialist in bariatric medicine and theirs is a woodsey lair.

4135 Woodland Brook Drive

Located on a wooded, twenty-five-acre Chattahoochee River estate, this French provincial-style house has been home to three families since its completion in 1974. First credit for this estate goes to Mr. and Mrs. William A. Rooker Jr., who assembled the property along the Cobb County bank of the Chattahoochee, as well as an experienced team of experts that included architect James "Jimmy" Means (1904-79), landscape architect William "Billy" Monroe (1927-99), builder Byron Parker and millworker Jim Girdler.

Approached by a winding drive through forested and naturalistically landscaped property, with glimpses on the east of Chattahoochee white-water rapids, the balanced cream stucco pavilion comes into view as one enters a gravel forecourt bordered by cobblestones. (See page 13.) The present owners, James and Rebekah Warren, purchased this private hideaway in August 1996. Panoramic views of a landscaped flood plain and white water in the distance are part of every room on the riverside, with French doors on the first floor opening onto a deep terrace.

James Warren found the house in April 1996 through his own builder, Brad Hodges, when it was owned by Mr. and Mrs. Don Sentell and when he was looking for land on which to build his own home. He read a Harry Norman, Realtors' flyer, which mentioned James Means and William Monroe, and set out to learn more about Means. (Mrs. Monroe is a cousin of his father.)

After they acquired the house the Warrens added solid French exterior shutters shown on the original working drawings Means made for the Rookers. The young couple considers a major aspect of the value of their home to be the way it was created by the Rookers' team, and they intend to preserve the beauty of the place they have fallen heir to whenever they make necessary modifications as they raise their family here. They consider it their "homeplace," to use an old Georgia term.

Current owners: Mr. and Mrs. James K. Warren

Completed in 1974 for the William Rookers by architect James Means, the youthful owners respect the history of the place as they have renovated it in the 1990s to suit their present needs. The style is classic French provincial, as only Jimmy Means could do in our day.

161

2865 Camp Branch Road
Holly Hill

The 1936 novel *Gone with the Wind* and the film based on it captured the world's imagination, focusing attention on the life and culture of antebellum Georgia and its aftermath. People identified the homes Tara and Twelve Oaks as central to that story. Just like Vivian Leigh and Clark Gable, the houses became stars.

People continued to keep alive the idea of classical houses as the most appropriate kind of home for Georgians. In 1951 the book *White Columns in Georgia* perpetuated the notion that the true Georgian way was a large classical front porch. In 1968 the state of Georgia completed a new governor's mansion, which is surrounded by thirty Doric columns twenty-four feet high. Then in the 1970s and '80s came a new interest in architectural traditions as a source of contemporary design and in historic preservation as well.

Part of this trend toward a revived classicism, a love of history and old houses, is this great columned house that Mr. and Mrs. James E. Hinshaw Sr. completed as their home in 1985. In Gwinnett County near Buford, the estate originally had thirty acres; the current owners, Bahallah and Herb Newton, have added thirty more. The home was modeled after an 1830s plantation house from Queen Anne's County, on the eastern shore of Maryland. Called Blakeford, a Southern house in form and lifestyle, it was illustrated in *The Golden Treasury of Early American Homes* (1967), by Richard Pratt. (Blakeford no longer stands.) The designer and builder Jim Strickland drew plans based on the photographs in a copy of Pratt's book.

This house fits into a pattern of romantic classicism that goes back still further than the houses of the 1830s, '40s, and '50s of the plantation South – into the eighteenth century and even to the designs of the sixteenth-century Italian Renaissance architect Andrea Palladio, who based his designs on the rural villas of ancient Rome. This is a country villa sited on an estate reminiscent of the expansive English naturalistic landscapes designed with pleasure gardens and specimen plants and trees, a lake, gazebo, chapel, guesthouse, and other structures completing the picture of a working but aristocratic plantation.

Current owners: Herb and Bahallah Newton

155 Greenville Street

Founded in 1827 and located forty miles southwest of Atlanta, Newnan was named for a War of 1812 veteran, Gen. Daniel Newnan. It is the seat of Coweta County, which was named for the Creek Indian "Coweta Towns" that were in the area prior to 1825. Newnan has long been known as a prosperous manufacturing center, especially for textiles, and as an affluent and cultivated town of fine schools and beautiful homes. Newnan has had three of its historic districts listed on the National Register of Historic Places. Its historic downtown, surrounding the refurbished county courthouse, has been revitalized under the national Main Street program. One of the landmarks in this city of beautiful and historic homes is this extraordinary Second Empire-style mansion built in 1886 on Greenville Street. It has been called the Parrott-Camp-Soucy house since the Soucys restored it over a period of two years in the mid 1980s. It is on the National Register, and the Georgia Trust for Historic Preservation honored the Soucys' exceptional work with an Outstanding Restoration Award in 1986.

The Soucys' labor-of-love restoration included extensive repairs because of termite damage, a leaking mansard roof of multicolored slates, crumbling plasterwork, too many coats of paint inside and out, dangerous old wiring, and many more problems. Layers of white paint were removed from the exterior, which was repainted in its original Victorian period colors – five shades of gray. Central heat and air were installed. The floors were cleaned and treated with coats of hand-applied tung oil. Originally, each room on the first floor had been trimmed in a different wood, which is now carefully restored: mahogany in the parlor, cherry in the dining room, pine in the kitchen, and walnut in the master bedroom. Original light fixtures downstairs were cleaned and repaired; upstairs, missing light fixtures now have authentic replacements. Finally, it was meticulously furnished in the style of the 1880s.

Mr. and Mrs. Rick Cousins are the fortunate current owners of Newnan's favorite Victorian house restoration, a veritable museum of period architecture and interior decoration, as well. It is now truly entitled to be called the Parrott-Camp-Soucy-Cousins home.

Current owners: Mr. and Mrs. Richard Cousins

In the mid-1880s, an earlier house that stood on this site was remodeled in the Second Empire style. Restored and furnished a century later to its 1880s appearance, the Parrot-Camp-Soucy-Cousins home is like a house museum in quality.

101 Bill Hart Road

This extraordinary restoration project included moving the endangered 1830s house from LaGrange, Georgia, to this six-acre site on the outskirts of Newnan. Miles Whitfield, an architect who specializes in restorations, found out about this land from the Newnan antiquarian William Banks, who had also moved and restored a house of about the same vintage and style.

Whitfield purchased the house in 1996 and had it moved in August of that year. Its original site had been 612 Hines Street in a part of LaGrange that had become entirely commercial, and the property had been so zoned. After the death of Sarah Render Wilcox, who had held out there to the bitter end in her family's homeplace, its future was decidedly uncertain. Whitfield stepped in to save it by moving it to a knoll on his Coweta County property, similar to its original site. He wanted to make the old house new, but seem old and at home on its new site.

Everyone with a knowledge of old Georgia houses knew the Magnolias, as it had long been called, or sometimes the Render House. It had actually been built for Joseph D. McFarland about 1833 by the builder-architect Collin Rodgers (1791-1845) in the transitional federal-Greek revival style for which Rodgers is known. His houses all had pedimented porticoes with four fluted Ionic columns, as well as fanlights over entrance doorways leading into wide central halls. All were frame with clapboarding but with flush siding on the wall under the portico. This house is considered to be Rodgers's only story-and-a-half. Because of its architectural importance the Magnolias was documented by the Historic American Buildings Survey in 1934.

Miles Whitfield aspired to an accurate restoration of his truly landmark home; he had paint and wallpaper studies done to determine what had been there originally to help him recreate an authentic 1830s house from the ceiling, to the floors, to all the details of furnishings and art works. The October 1999 Southern issue of *House Beautiful* magazine has his home on the cover, followed by a seven-page illustrated article worthy of the private house-museum he has fashioned in Coweta County.

Current owner: Miles Gandy Whitfield

The architect-owner saved this LaGrange landmark by moving it to a new site near Newnan and carefully restoring and furnishing it to its original 1830s appearance.

507 South Main Street

Madison, founded in 1809, was described forty years later by the Reverend George White as the "wealthiest and most aristocratic village along the stagecoach route between Charleston and New Orleans." In our own era, Madison, the county seat of Morgan County, is near I-20 East and less than an hour from Atlanta.

Madison is still affluent and genteel, as it was in the days of antebellum cotton. As that era was ending, a Connecticut Yankee sergeant passed through with the Federal troops who did not entirely burn the place (only valuable railroad facilities, the depot, cotton warehouses, cotton, and Confederate supplies). On that day, November 19, 1864, Sergeant Mead wrote: "Madison is the prettiest village I've seen in the state. One garden and yard I never saw excelled, even in Connecticut." Perhaps its beauty helped to save it, and it's still a saving grace for Madison, which is a happily and successfully historic preservation-minded town.

Number 507 South Main Street was there in the mid-nineteenth century. The house we know today was remodeled later in the century during the neoclassical revival movement, which sought to identify with the antebellum classicism of the Greek and Roman revivals but not to duplicate them exactly. The six fluted white columns in the Roman composite order were rarely seen in Georgia before this turn-of-the-century remodeling; also characteristic of that second-period remodeling is the hipped dormer on the roof and the one-over-one single-pane window sashes.

This large, shining white-and-black house certainly contributes great presence to Madison's historic district, projects affluence and aristocratic heritage, and helps to uphold the town's warranted reputation as an outstandingly pretty village.

Current owners: Sam and Cecilia Hendrix

35 Rome Road

Fifteen miles south of Rome and one hour north of Atlanta, Cave Spring is a picturesque village settled in 1829 in Vann's Valley. A multiple resources study of this well-preserved, special place resulted in some ninety structures being included in a listing on the National Register of Historic Places. One of them is this brick house on the Rome Road near Little Cedar Creek. Built between 1845 and 1848, and long known as the William Cowdry plantation, it has been carefully renovated and was a Georgia Trust for Historic Preservation award winner. A historic country classical home, it not surprisingly has eight fireplaces, but it also has a hot tub, swimming pool, fancy billiard table, and three-car garage.

Cave Spring's namesake mineral spring, flowing from a limestone cave in a twenty-nine-acre park in the middle of town, feeds Little Cedar Creek, which flows by this house. The mineral spring has a capacity of about four million gallons of pure water a day, a portion of which is now being bottled and sold commercially.

Cave Spring's limestone cave and spring boast a summer temperature of 56 degrees. Because Cave Spring is naturally air conditioned, it is no wonder that this house has such unusually wide, welcoming verandahs to take in the north Georgia breezes wafting from the spring and nearby creek.

Current owners: Doc and Ginny Kibler

The broad wraparound verandahs of this country Greek revival mansion are well designed for shade and prevailing breezes, as one relaxes and sips "branch water" from the nearby spring-fed creek.

Glen Mary Plantation

The accomplished historical architect Edward Vason Jones (1909-80) photographed this house many times in the late 1930s and in the 1940s, once in early Kodachrome, in his travels around the backwoods and byways of the state. Later, in the 1960s, he was involved as a consultant in restoration work there for the longtime owners, Miss Elizabeth Nichols and Mrs. James F. Nichols, relatives of Gen. and Mrs. Ethan A. Hitchcock, who purchased it in 1869.

Glen Mary was built about 1853 by Theophilus Jackson Smith on the Linton Road, south of Sparta. One writer has called it a high-style Greek revival cottage and says it rises grandly on its hill above the countryside like a Greek temple on a small acropolis. On this site its deep, shaded columned porch raised above stout ground floor piers, of course, takes advantage of any breezes and provides vistas. The thick walls of the basement floor and the high ceilings of the main floor help with natural air conditioning, as do the large windows and doors.

Glen Mary has a rich interior: "cranberry" glass in the transom and sidelights of the principal entrance door of the main floor casts a friendly glow in the wide hallway, enriched further with exceptional ornamental plasterwork, signed by a plasterer, Francis McDermott. (Edward Jones and his expert crew restored this plasterwork for the Nichols family and used molds from it to enrich a display room at the Metropolitan Museum of Art during its Nineteenth Century Show in 1970.)

Glen Mary is listed on the National Register of Historic Places. Restoration continues under the directon of Mrs. Marilyn Meyers, who is researching the exact appearance of both the front and rear of the historic home. The classical Doric colonnade, forming a full length piazza, was originally reached by a staircase that has disappeared and has only been temporarily replaced.

Current owner: Preservation America Foundation
             Mrs. Marilyn Meyers, Chief Trustee

Built in 1853 in the Greek revival style, Glen Mary has a particularly rich interior. The current owner is continuing the restoration begun in the 1960s by the late Edward Vason Jones who admired this house above almost all other Greek revival houses in the state. Jones was an accomplished architect and a consultant to the Metropolitan Museum of Art, the White House and the U.S. State Department.

Index

Acknowledgements

AUTHOR'S ACKNOWLEDGEMENTS
Harry and Amy Norman, Lynne Smith, Jane Powers Weldon, Linda Williams, Nancy Moseley, Andy Sirmon, Ross Butler, Caroline Coles, Norman Askins, Southern Architecture Foundation, Inc. Board of Directors and Executive Committee: James K. Warren, Marion Slaton and Boyd Coons, Homeowners past and present, Miriam H. Mitchell

Photo Credits

ROBERT THIEN: Dust jacket photos, Front and back endpapers, Pages 1, 2, 5, 6, 7 (top), 14-15, 22-23, 24-25, 32-33, 34-35, 36-37, 38-39, 42-43, 44-47, 52-53, 56-57, 58-59, 60-61, 64-65, 68-69, 70-73, 80-81, 82-83, 84-87, 88-89, 92-93, 94-95, 98-99, 100-101, 106-109, 110-111, 116-117, 123, 124-125 (bottom), 126-127, 128-129, 134-135, 136-138, 140-141, 142-143, 150-151, 152-153, 154-157, 172-173

DEBORAH WHITLAW: Pages 7 (bottom), 13, 16-19, 20-21, 26-27, 28-29, 30-31, 40-41, 48-49, 50-51, 54-55, 66-67, 74-75, 76-77, 78-79, 90-91, 96-97, 102-103, 104-105, 112-115, 118-121, 130-133, 146-147, 148-149, 158-159, 160-161, 164-165, 170-171

LUIS MENDOZA: Pages 8, 9, 10, 62-63, 125 (top), 144-145, 162, 166-167, 168-169, 176

RAY BOULEY: Page 11, 122

DAVE DAWSON: Page 139

RICK TOMLIN: Page 163

SUPPLIED BY OWNER: Page 84 (bottom)